English G 21

Klassenarbeitstrainer

für Schülerinnen und Schüler

mit Lösungen und Lerntipps

English G 21 • Band 1

Klassenarbeitstrainer mit Lösungen und Lerntipps

Erarbeitet von
Dr. Ursula Mulla und Nogi Mulla, Germering

In Zusammenarbeit mit der Englischredaktion
Dr. Christiane Kallenbach (Projektleitung)
Julie Colthorpe
Ursula Fleischhauer
Britta Bensmann (Bildredaktion)

Beratende Mitwirkung
Wolfgang Biederstädt, Köln
Martina Schroeder, Stedtlingen
Bernd Sold, Bobenheim-Roxheim
Udo Wagner, Voerde

Illustrationen
Constanze Schargan, Berlin

Bildquellen
Alamy, Abingdon (S. 27 Jessica Summer: geogphotos; S. 66 Bild A: Jeff Morgan heritage; S. 79 pool: kolvenbach, park:
ACE STOCK LIMITED, farm: Image Source Black, museum: Yadid Levy); Bristol City Council Photo Library, Bristol (S. 66 Bild C);
Rob Cousins, Bristol (S. 18 classroom); Nathalie Schwering, Berlin (S. 27 Grandma and Grandpa Scott); Shutterstock, New York
(S. 27 Grandma Summer: iofoto, Grandpa Summer: Kruchankova Maya, Eileen Scott: Hallgerd, Bob Scott: Brenda Arlene
Smith, Mary Summer: rj lerich, Joe Summer: Lisa F. Young, Jacob Scott: Alexey Avdeev, Luke Summer: Gnuskin Petr; S. 66
Bild B: Bateleur); Hartmut Tschepe, Berlin (S. 27 Jane, Herbert u. Andrea Kiefer, Emma Scott)

Titelbild
Constanze Schargan, Berlin; IFA-Bilderteam, Ottobrunn (Hintergrund Union Jack: Jon Arnold Images)

Layout und technische Umsetzung
Heike Freund, Hameln

Umschlaggestaltung
Klein & Halm Grafikdesign, Berlin

www.cornelsen.de
www.EnglishG.de

1. Auflage, 3. Druck 2009

© 2008 Cornelsen Verlag, Berlin

Druck: CS-Druck CornelsenStürtz, Berlin

ISBN 978-3-06-031949-7 (B1)   978-3-06-031950-3 (D1)

 Inhalt gedruckt auf säurefreiem Papier aus nachhaltiger Forstwirtschaft.

INHALT

VORWORT

Liebe Schülerin, lieber Schüler,

du willst dich in diesem Schuljahr auf Klassenarbeiten und mündliche Prüfungen im Fach Englisch gut vorbereiten. Der **Klassenarbeitstrainer** hilft dir dabei. Er enthält zu jeder Unit deines Englischbuches zwei Klassenarbeiten, in denen du die **Fertigkeiten (skills)** Listening, Reading, Writing und Getting by in English sowie Speaking trainieren kannst. Das **Inhaltsverzeichnis** zeigt dir, wo du die Klassenarbeiten und die **Speaking**-Aufgaben findest.

Das **Lösungsheft** hilft dir, deine Klassenarbeiten zu überprüfen. Dort findest du auch die abgedruckten **Texte** zu den Listening-Aufgaben und viele **Lerntipps**.
Mit dem **Bewertungsschlüssel** in der Umschlaginnenseite kannst du deine Leistung einschätzen und zu deiner Gesamtpunktzahl die entsprechende Note finden.

☞ Listening Aufgaben
Lies dir zuerst die Überschrift und den Aufgabenteil in Ruhe durch. Dann weißt du, um welches Thema es geht. Höre dir anschließend den Listening-Text auf der **CD** an. Konzentriere dich nur auf das Hören. Stelle dir die Sprecher/innen und das, worüber sie sprechen, in Bildern vor. Höre weiter zu, auch wenn du etwas nicht verstanden hast. Bearbeite dann die Aufgaben, die du schon bearbeiten kannst. Höre dir den Listening-Text ein zweites Mal an. Konzentriere dich auf Stellen, die dir helfen, Aufgaben zu bearbeiten, bei denen du unsicher warst. Bearbeite nun die noch fehlenden Aufgaben.

☞ Reading Aufgaben
Lies dir die Überschrift und den Text in Ruhe durch. Stelle dir in Bildern vor, was im Text steht. Mache ein Fragezeichen an den Rand, wo dir etwas unklar ist. Fasse für dich in einem Satz zusammen, worum es in diesem Text geht. Lies dann die Aufgaben zum Text, ohne sie zu bearbeiten. Jetzt weißt du, worauf du im Text besonders achten musst. Lies nun den Text ein zweites Mal. Unterstreiche Informationen, die dir bei der Bearbeitung der Aufgaben helfen. Nimm dabei für jede Aufgabe eine andere Farbe. Bearbeite dann die Aufgaben. Achte genau auf die Aufgabenstellung und suche im Text die Stellen, die für diese Aufgabe wichtig sind.

☞ Writing Aufgaben und Aufgaben zu Getting by in English
Lies dir die Aufgabe in Ruhe durch. Du kannst in Stichpunkten notieren, was du schreiben möchtest. Beachte dabei die Hilfestellung, die dir angeboten wird. Schreibe dann deinen Text. Lies dir deinen Text durch und überprüfe, ob du alle Aufgabenteile erfüllt hast, ob deine englischen Sätze richtig klingen und ob du die einzelnen Wörter richtig geschrieben hast.

☞ Speaking Aufgaben
Lies zuerst die Aufgabenstellung. Höre dir dann auf der **CD** den Musterdialog an. Du kannst das auch mehrere Male tun und dabei schon mitsprechen. Dann bist du fit für deinen eigenen Sprechbeitrag.

Für dieses Schuljahr wünschen wir dir viel Erfolg und Freude.

Dr. Ursula und Nogi Mulla

Gesamtpunktzahl _______ / 65   Note _______

LISTENING

_______ / 15

 **01 Hi!**

Höre Jessica, Luke und David zweimal zu und ergänze dann die Tabelle.

☞ Lies im Vorwort, S. 4, wie du **Listening**-Aufgaben gut lösen kannst.
Du kannst diese Aufgabe auch als **Reading**-Aufgabe machen.
Lies dazu den Text im **Lösungsheft**, S. 2, und bearbeite dann die Aufgabe.

1   Where are they from?

_______ / 3

Tick (✔) the right box.

	Bristol	London
Jessica is from		
Luke is from		
David is from		

2   How old are they?

_______ / 3

Tick (✔) the right box.

	eleven	twelve
Jessica is		
Luke is		
David is		

Jessica, Luke and David

_______ / 9

Ergänze die Tabelle. Antworte mit einem Wort.

Name	Jessica	Luke	David
Their favourite colour?			
The colour of their school bag?			
Their favourite day?			

LANGUAGE

_____ / 30

1　WORDS Luke's calendar

_____ / 5

Write the days. Schreibe die Wochentage.

Monday
football training

T____________________
shopping with Mum

W____________________
help Dad

T____________________
5:45 Doctor Brown

F____________________
party

____________day / Sunday
Weekend!!!

2　WORDS What's the time?

_____ / 5

Match the clocks and the times. Ordne den Uhren die richtige Zeit zu.

1　It's quarter to nine.

2　It's half past ten.

3　It's twelve fifty.

4　It's two twenty-five.

5　It's four forty.

6　It's ten past six.

☞　**Analoge Uhrzeiten:** Du verwendest **past** oder **to** ▶ quarter to; half past
Digitale Uhrzeiten: Du nennst zuerst die Stunde, dann die Minuten.

3 GRAMMAR You and the kids in your school book

_____/5

Complete the sentences. Ergänze die Sätze.

☞ I'm (2x) • He's (2x) • She's (4x) • They're (2x)

1 This is Ananda Kapoor.

_______________ eleven years old.

_______________ from Bristol.

2 This is Jack Hanson.

_______________ eleven years old.

_______________ from Bristol.

3 This is Sophie Carter-Brown.

_______________ eleven years old.

_______________ new in Bristol.

4 This is Dan Shaw with his twin brother Jo.

_______________ twins.

_______________ from Bristol.

AND YOU?

5 My name is _____________________________. _____________________ years old.

_______________ from ____.

4 GRAMMAR Dan and you

_____/10

Find the questions. Lies Dans Antworten und schreibe deine Fragen auf.

☞ **Fragewörter:** How • What (3x) • Where

1 name?

You ____ *Dan* My name is Dan Shaw.

2 old?

You ____ *Dan* I'm twelve.

3 from?

You ____ *Dan* I'm from Bristol.

4 favourite colour?

You ____ *Dan* My favourite colour is blue.

5 colour / pencil case?

You ____ *Dan* My pencil case is blue.

5 WORDS Late for school

_____ / 5

Complete the dialogues. Ergänze die Dialoge. Verwende folgende Ausdrücke:

> excuse me • me too • sorry • that's right • you're welcome

1 *Jack* ________________________________,

what's the time, please?

Mrs Schmidt It's ten to nine.

Jack Thank you, Mrs Schmidt.

Mrs Schmidt ________________________________.

2 *Jack* I think we're in room 14 now.

Dan Yes, ________________________________.

Jack I'm late.

Dan ________________________________.

3 *Mr Kingsley* It's ten past nine. Jack, Dan.

You're late!

Jack and Dan ________________________________, sir.

WRITING

_____ / 20

Who am I?

Schreibe über dich. Die Mindmap hilft dir.

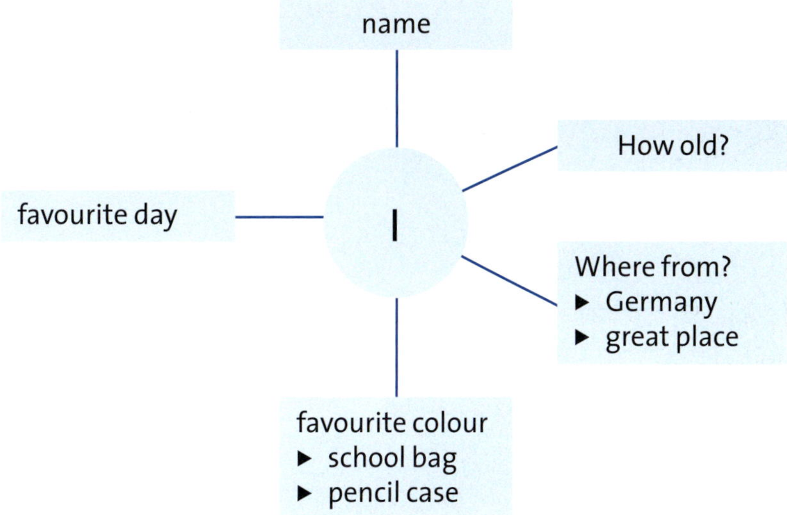

Hi,

My name ____

 So kannst du deine Sätze beginnen:
I'm …
It's …
My favourite colour / day …
My school bag …

Welcome   Klassenarbeit B

Gesamtpunktzahl _________ / 65   Note _______

READING

_________ / 15

Jessica and Luke's shopping list

Jessica and Luke Summer live in Bristol with their mum and dad. Today is the last day of the summer holidays.

Mrs Summer	Jessica! Luke! What about your shopping list for school?
Jessica	I need a new school bag, Mum.
Mrs Summer	A new school bag? What about your old school bag, Jessica?
Jessica	It's old and it's pink.
5 *Mrs Summer*	Pink is a nice colour for girls.
Jessica	But pink isn't a nice colour for a school bag.
Mrs Summer	What is a nice colour for a school bag?
Jessica	Black.
Mrs Summer	Black! No, Jessica, not a black school bag. Black isn't a nice colour for a girl.
10 *Luke*	Mum, I need a new school bag too. My school bag is old and it's black.
Mrs Summer	Oh, Luke! Your school bag isn't old and black is a nice colour for boys. What about exercise books, pencils, glue sticks, and rulers?
Luke	I need four exercise books and a new pencil case.
Mrs Summer	Where is your old pencil case, Luke?
15 *Luke*	I can't find it.
Mrs Summer	And you need a new pen, new pencils and new felt tips.
Luke	Yes, and a glue stick.
Mrs Summer	Oh Luke! What about you, Jessica?
Jessica	My pencil case is OK, but I need a new glue stick too.
20 *Mrs Summer*	What about exercise books?
Jessica	I need five exercise books.
Mrs Summer	That's five exercise books for you, Jessica. Four exercise books for Luke. A pencil case with a new pen, new pencils and new felt tips for Luke and two glue sticks. No rulers?
25 *Jessica*	That's right, Mum. No new rulers, but two new school bags.
Mrs Summer	No, Jessica no new school bag for you and no new school bag for you, Luke.

1 Right – Wrong – Not in the text?

_____ / 5

Tick (✔) the correct box.

	Right	Wrong	Not in the text
1 Jessica is Luke's sister.			
2 Jessica and Luke are in Form 7.			
3 Jessica's school bag is black.			
4 Her pencil case is pink.			
5 Luke's school bag is black.			

2 Is it on Mrs Summer's shopping list? Yes _or_ No?

_____ / 10

Schau dir die Liste an und mache ein Häkchen ✔ in das richtige Kästchen.

	Yes	No
1 school bag		
2 pencil case		
3 two pens		
4 one pen		
5 ruler		
6 four exercise books		
7 nine exercise books		
8 two glue sticks		
9 one glue stick		
10 pencils		

LANGUAGE

_____ / 30

1 WORDS Five pencils – five colours

_____ / 5

Write the colour. Schreibe die Farbe auf.

My pencils are:

1 ____

2 ____

3 ____

4 ____

5 ____

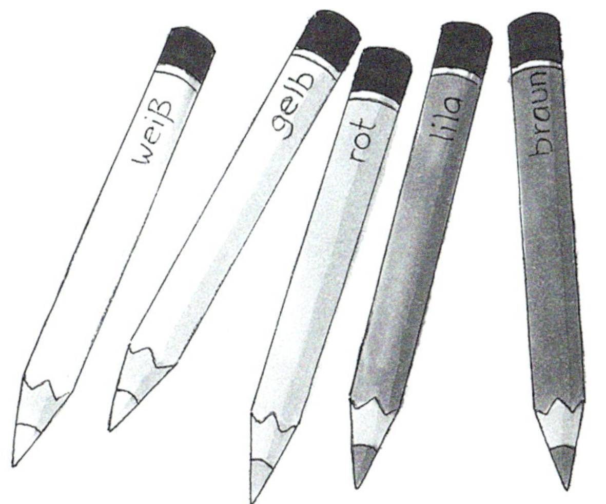

2 WORDS Luke

_____ / 5

Find the opposite. Finde das Gegenteil.

1 I'm not a <u>girl</u>. I'm a ___________________, of course.

2 My school bag isn't ___________________. It's <u>old</u>.

3 My school bag is ___________________. It isn't <u>full</u>.

4 You can <u>open</u> my school bag, and I can ___________________ it.

5 I can't ___________________ this box, but I can <u>push</u> it.

3 WORDS Twins in Form[1] 7JM

_____ / 5

Fill in. Ergänze. Verwende folgende Wörter:

my (2x) • your (2x) • his (2x) • her • our (2x) • their

1 **Sophie**   Hi, ___________ name is Sophie Carter-Brown. What's ___________ name?

   Jessica   Jessica. Jessica Summer and that's my twin brother. ___________ name is Luke.

2 **Sophie**   Who is ___________ English teacher?

   Jessica   Mr Morton. He is ___________ form teacher too. We are in Form 7JM.

3 **Sophie**   Jo, Dan! Come here. That's Jessica and that's ___________ brother, Luke.

      They're twins too. ___________ English teacher is Mr Morton. They're in Form 7JM.

   Jo   Hi Jessica! Hi Luke! You're the twins in 7JM and we are the twins in Form 7PK.

      That's ___________ form!

4 **Jessica**   Who's Dan and who's Jo?

   Jo   I'm Jo and this is Dan. I'm ___________ brother and he's ___________ twin brother.

4 SOUNDS Dan's trick with words

_____ / 5

Odd word out. Sprich und höre, welches Wort nicht in die Reihe passt.

1 great – teacher – eight   ___________________________________

2 summer – you – double   ___________________________________

3 who – two – good   ___________________________________

4 here – there – their   ___________________________________

5 nice – kite – day   ___________________________________

[1] form [fɔːm] _Klasse_

5 WORDS We are late!

_____ / 5

Write the time. Schreibe auf, wie spät es ist.

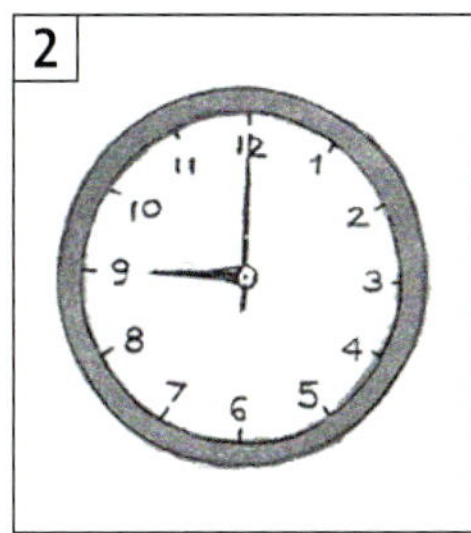

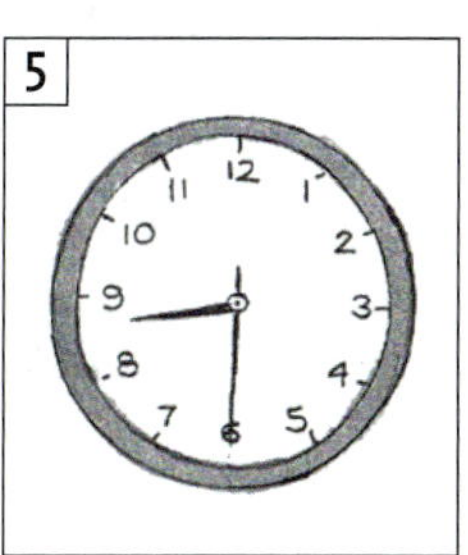

1 *Mr Summer* Oh no! It's ________________________________. I'm late for work.

2 *Jessica* Oh no! It's ________________________________. I'm late for school.

3 *Luke* Oh no! It's ________________________________. I'm late for football.

4 *Grandma* Oh no! It's ________________________________. I'm late for my TV show.

5 *Mrs Summer* Oh no! It's ________________________________. I'm late for the party.

> **Digitale Uhrzeiten:** Nenne zuerst die Stunde, dann die Minuten.
> **Analoge Uhrzeiten:** Du verwendest **to** oder **past** ▶ ten to …; twenty past …

6 WORDS How old are they?

_____ / 5

1 Charlie is *five*.

2 Mia and Sue are ________________.

3 Mr Scott is ________________.

4 Mrs Scott is ________________.

5 Her car is ________________ years old.

6 Emma is ________________.

7 Her brother Jacob is ________________.

8 Mary is ________________.

9 Grandpa Scott is ________________.

10 Our cat is ________________.

11 And our house is ________________ years old.

WRITING

_____ / 20

The things in my school bag

Ergänze die Mindmap mit drei Dingen, die du in deiner Schultasche und vier Dingen, die du in deinem Federmäppchen hast. Schreibe auf, welche Farbe sie haben, z. B. a pencil case, purple; a rubber, blue.

Schreibe jetzt, was du in deiner Schultasche hast.

In my school bag I've got ____

In my pencil case I've got ____

Klassenarbeit A

Unit 1

Gesamtpunktzahl _______ / 60   Note _______

READING

_______ / 15

Jo's e-mail to his mum

▶ sue.shaw@yahoo.com

Hi Dan, hi Jo,

Your first week at your new school! Have you got nice teachers and nice classmates? Is everything OK at home? Here everything is OK. Good luck to you. Please write!

5 Love, Mum

▶ JoShaw@hotmail.co.uk

Hi Mum,

School is OK. I like PE, but English isn't my favourite subject. Our PE teacher is our English teacher too. His name is Mr Kingsley. He is our form teacher. Then there is Mr Barker, our Geography teacher. Jack thinks
10 he has got a face like a bank robber, but Jack has got mad ideas. Jack is my new friend. There are girls in our form too. There is Ananda. She is a good hockey player[1] and she likes Maths.
Dad is at work and Dan is in the kitchen[2]. He can't make tea and he can't make nice sandwiches, but it's his turn in the kitchen today. It's good we can eat at school. The food there is OK. But your food is the best[3]! How is everything in New Zealand?

15 Love, Jo

1   This is what Jo likes

_______ / 5

Tick (✔) Yes or No.

Jo likes ...	Yes	No
1 ... PE		
2 ... English		
3 ... Jack		
4 ... Dan's sandwiches		
5 ... Mum's food		

[1] player [ˈpleɪə] *Spieler/in*   [2] kitchen [ˈkɪtʃɪn] *Küche*   [3] the best [best] *das Beste*

2   Right – Wrong – Not in the text?

_____ / 10

Tick (✔) the correct box.

		Right	Wrong	Not in the text
1	School is OK for Jo.	☐	☐	☐
2	School is OK for Dan.	☐	☐	☐
3	Mr Kingsley is a good teacher.	☐	☐	☐
4	He's Jo's form teacher.	☐	☐	☐
5	He looks like a bank robber.	☐	☐	☐
6	Mr Barker is Jo's Geography teacher.	☐	☐	☐
7	Jack is Dan's friend.	☐	☐	☐
8	Ananda can play hockey.	☐	☐	☐
9	Dan is in the kitchen.	☐	☐	☐
10	Jo's dad is in the kitchen too.	☐	☐	☐

LANGUAGE

_____ / 25

1   GRAMMAR New friends

_____ / 5

*Ergänze eine Form von **(to) be** und, wo nötig, ein Personalpronomen.*

1 *Luke*   Hi, I _________________ Luke and who _________________ you?

2 *Dan*   _________________ Dan. This is Jo. _________________ my brother.

3 *Luke*   _________________ you twins?

   Dan   Yes, we are.

4 *Jo*   Where are Sophie and Ananda?

5 *Dan*   _________________ are in Dilip's classroom.

6 *Luke*   Who _________________ Sophie and Ananda?

7 *Jo*   _________________ my friends.

   Luke   And who is Dilip?

8 *Dan*   _________________ Ananda's brother.

9 *Luke*   Where is your classroom?

10 *Jo*   _________________ here.

 Bei dieser Übung geht es um Personalpronomen **(personal pronouns):**
I, you, he, she, it, we, you, they

Zu jedem Personalpronomen gehört eine Form von **(to) be: am, is, are**
Und so gehören sie richtig zusammen: **I ▸ am** und **he / she / it ▸ is**
alle anderen Personalpronomen **▸ are**

2 GRAMMAR Short answers

_____/5

*Write short answers to the **be**, **can** and **have** questions. Use the right verb.*

1 Is Mr Kingsley a teacher?   Yes, ______________________________.

2 Are Dan and Jo twins?   Yes, ______________________________.

3 Has Jack got a parrot?   Yes, ______________________________.

4 Has he got a brother?   No, ______________________________.

5 Can Polly swim?   No, ______________________________.

6 Can Polly say 'Good morning'?   Yes, ______________________________.

7 Is Toby a dog?   No, ______________________________.

8 Is he Sophie's brother?   Yes, ______________________________.

9 Are you ten?   ____.

10 Can you sing?   ____.

3 GRAMMAR What have they got? What haven't they got?

_____/5

Look at the pictures and complete the sentences. Schau dir die Bilder an und ergänze die Sätze.

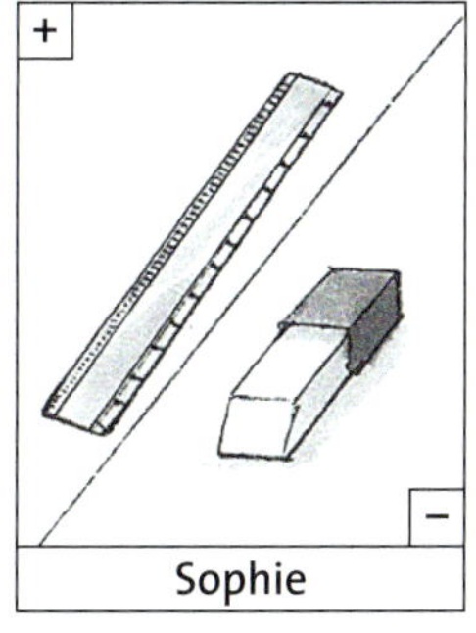
Sophie

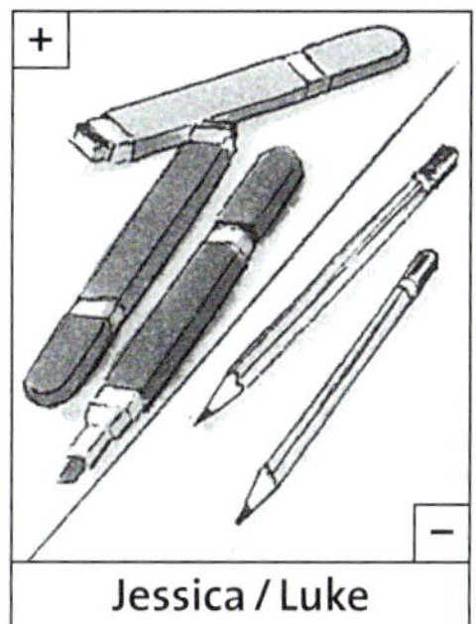
Jessica / Luke

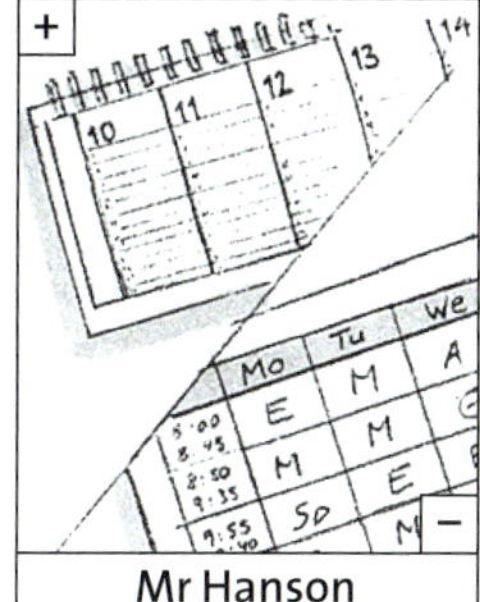
Mr Hanson

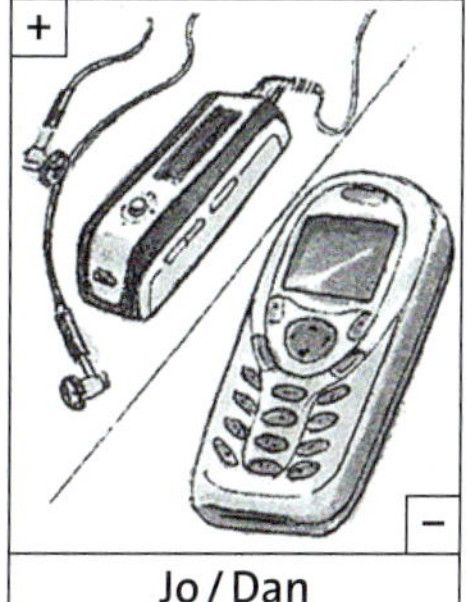
Jo / Dan

Ananda

1 *Has* Sophie got a ruler? Yes, she ________. But she *hasn't got* ______________________________.

2 *Have* Jessica and Luke ________ felt tips? Yes, they ________. But ______________________________.

3 ________ Mr Hanson got a timetable? No, he ________. But ______________________________.

4 ________ Jo and Dan ________ an MP3 player?

   Yes, ______________. But ______________________________.

5 ______________________ a banana? Yes, she ________. But ______________________________.

 **have got / has got**

So bildest du **Fragen**:	So bildest du **Kurzantworten**:	So bildest du **Verneinungen**:
Has she **got** …?	**Yes** she **has**. / **No** he **hasn't**.	She **hasn't got** …
Have they **got** …?	**Yes** they **have**. / **No** they **haven't**.	They **haven't got** …

4 GRAMMAR Do this! Don't do that!

_______ / 5

Was sagt Mr Kingsley? Was sollen die Kinder tun und was nicht?

> (✔) do • (✔) give • (✔) listen • (✔) look • (✔) open •
> (✔) read • (✔) take out • (✘) talk • (✔) tell • (✘) throw

1 _____________ me your names, please.

2 Jack, _____________ me your pencil, please, but _____________________________ it.

3 Now, _______________________ your English books and _____________ your books at page 29.

4 _____________ at the picture and _____________ exercise 10.

5 Dan and Jo, _______________________! _______________________ to me, please.

6 Ananda, _____________ sentence 1, please.

5 PRONUNCIATION 'a' or 'an'?

_______ / 5

Put the words in the right list. Schreibe die Wörter in die richtige Liste.

> red ruler • uniform • exercise book • yellow pen • idea •
> empty bag • apple • new word • joke • art lesson

a _______________________________   an _______________________________

a _______________________________   an _______________________________

a _______________________________   an _______________________________

a _______________________________   an _______________________________

a _______________________________   an _______________________________

WRITING

_____ / 20

Hi Mum

It's Tuesday and Jo is in the kitchen¹. Now Dan can write his mum a letter.
Write Dan's letter to his mum. The ideas can help you.

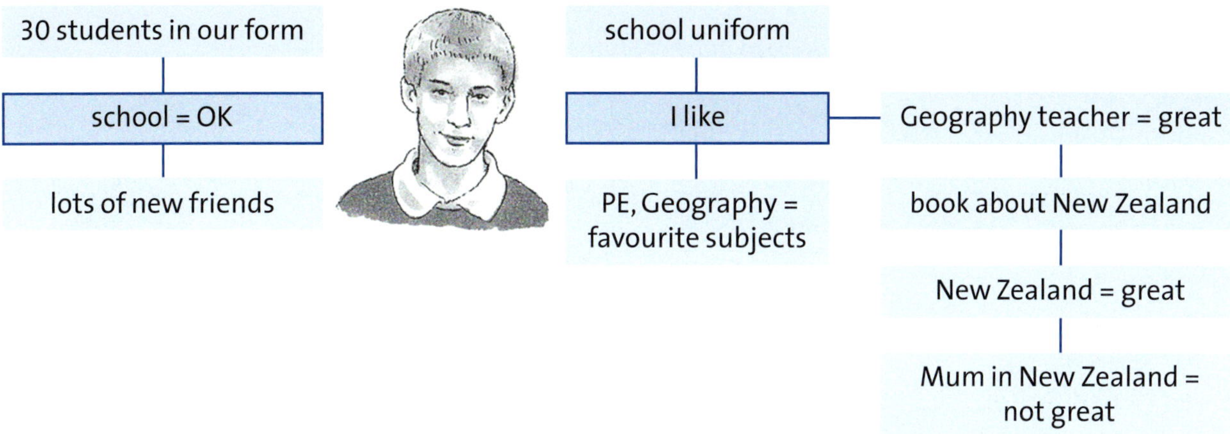

Start like this:

Hi Mum,

It is Jo's turn in the kitchen today and I can write to you about school and everything now. ____________________

 So kannst du deine Sätze beginnen:
Our new school ...
There are 30 students ...
I've got lots of ...
He has got a book ...
I think New Zealand ...

¹ kitchen ['kɪtʃɪn] *Küche*

Unit 1 — Klassenarbeit B

Gesamtpunktzahl _______ / 75   Note _______

LISTENING

_______ / 15

🎧 04 Lunch break at school

It's lunch break at school. Listen to Sarah Evans and her brother Sam.

☞ Du kannst diese Aufgabe auch als **Reading**-Aufgabe machen.
Den Text findest du auf Seite 10 im **Lösungsheft** abgedruckt.

1 Sam's timetable

_______ / 4

What are Sam's first lessons?

Monday	Tuesday	Wednesday	Thursday	Friday
Maths				

2 Sam's teachers and their subjects

_______ / 4

Tick (✔) the correct box.

Teachers	Form teacher	Maths	Science	History
Mr Hamilton				
Mrs Cooper				
Miss Smith				

3   Right or wrong?

_____/7

Tick (✔) the correct box.

		Right	Wrong
1	Sam's first day at school is OK.		
2	He likes Maths.		
3	He likes Miss Smith.		
4	Miss Smith is from India.		
5	He likes History.		
6	He likes Anna Schnitzer.		
7	He likes his timetable.		

LANGUAGE

_____/ 40

1   GRAMMAR Sarah Evans is in a wheelchair

_____/5

Ergänze eine Form von **(to) be** und, wo nötig, ein Personalpronomen.

1 **Sophie** _Are_ you Sarah Evans? _________________ Sophie Carter-Brown.

2 **Sarah** Yes, _________________. _________________ new here.

3 **Sophie** _________________ your timetable OK?

4 **Sarah** Well, _________________ OK, but I can't do sports at school.

5 **Sophie** _________________ the kids in your form nice?

6 **Sarah** Yes, _________________. Our teachers are nice too.

7 **Sophie** _________________ Mr Kingsley your English teacher?

8 **Sarah** No, _________________. Miss Taylor is our English teacher

and _________________ our form teacher too.

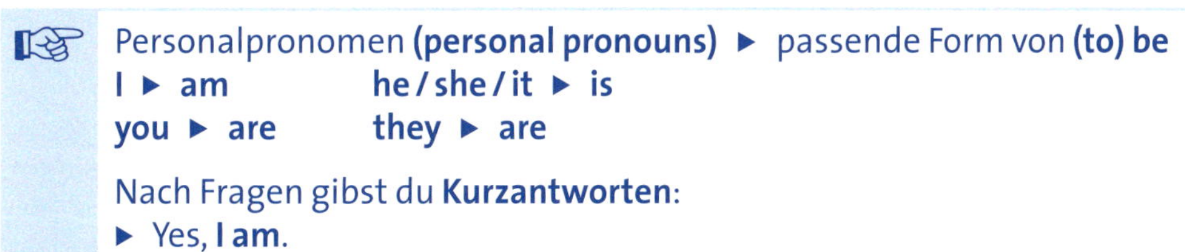

> ☞ Personalpronomen **(personal pronouns)** ▸ passende Form von **(to) be**
> I ▸ **am**   he / she / it ▸ **is**
> **you** ▸ **are**   **they** ▸ **are**
>
> Nach Fragen gibst du **Kurzantworten**:
> ▸ Yes, **I am.**
> ▸ No, **he isn't.**

2   GRAMMAR Questions for you   ____/5

Beantworte die Fragen. Verwende Kurzantworten.

1 *Sophie*   Are you from Germany?   *You*   Yes, ________________________________.

2 *Jo*   Are your friends from Germany too?   *You*   Yes, ________________________________.

3 *Dan*   Are you and your friends in Form 7?   *You*   No, _________________________________.

4 *Jack*   Is your English teacher nice?   *You*   ___________________________________.

5 *Dilip*   Is your school a big school?   *You*   ___________________________________.

3   GRAMMAR / WORDS What's there in Sam's room? What isn't there?   ____/10

Ergänze die Sätze mit

> there is • there are • is there • are there • there isn't • there aren't

1 ____________________ a table, but ____________________ a chair.

2 ____________________ a computer on his desk and ____________________ books on the floor.

3 ____________________ a football under his bed?   – No, ____________________.

4 ____________________ comics on his bed?   – Yes, ____________________.

5 ____________________ posters on the wall?   – No, ____________________.

4   GRAMMAR What have you got?

_____ / 10

Welche Dinge hast du, welche Dinge hast du nicht. Schreibe 5 Sätze.

1   I've got ________________, but I haven't got ________________ and I haven't got ________________.

2   I ________________________________, but ________________________

    and I haven't got ________________________.

3   I ________________, but ____.

4   I ________________, but ____.

5   I ________________, but ____.

5   GRAMMAR Do this! Don't do that!

_____ / 5

Was wollen sie von Sam? Ergänze ein Verb und **don't**, wenn nötig.

(✗) drop • (✔) have • (✔) meet • (✗) play • (✔) take

1   _Sarah_   Don't throw your things on my table and ____________ football with my school bag!

2   _Mrs Evans_   Hurry up, Sam, and ____________ this box to Mrs Kapoor, but ____________ it.

3   _Mrs Kapoor_   Come in, Sam. ____________ my friend Dinaz. She's from India.

4   _Dinaz_   Hi, Sam. Sit with us and ____________ a cup[1] of tea.

6   WORDS Birthdays

_____ / 5

Write their birthdays. Schreibe auf, wann sie Geburtstag haben.

1   _Sarah_   My birthday is on ________________________.

2   _Sam_   My birthday ________________________.

3   _Anna_   My ________________________.

4   _Jessica & Luke_ Our ________________________.

5   _You_   My ________________________.

Day	Month	Person
22	10	Sarah
3	3	Sam
15	12	Anna
31	7	Jessica & Luke
?	?	You

[1] cup [kʌp] _Tasse_

GETTING BY IN ENGLISH

_____ / 20

Anna Schnitzer's first day at school

Anna Schnitzers erster Tag an der englischen Schule ist aufregend. Wie kommt sie mit ihrem Englisch zurecht? Schreibe auf, was sie auf Englisch sagen muss, damit Sam sie versteht.

Anna grüßt Sam und stellt sich vor. (Name / neu hier / aus Deutschland)

Anna   ____

Sam   Hi, I'm Sam. Welcome to our form.

Anna will sagen, dass sie keinen Stuhl hat.

Anna   ____

Sam   Here you are. An empty chair for you.

Anna will fragen, ob sie sich dazusetzen darf.

Anna   ____

Sam   Yes, you can.

Anna will wissen, was sie als Nächstes haben.

Anna   ____

Sam   It's Maths with Mr Hamilton, then English with Miss Taylor in room 7.
After lunch break there is History in room 11 and then PE.

Anna will sagen, dass sie sich das nicht alles merken kann.

Anna   ____

Sam   Here's a timetable for you.

Anna will sich bedanken und sagen, dass deutsche Schulen anders sind als englische Schulen.

Anna   ____

Sam   What's different?

Anna will sagen, dass deutsche Schüler keine Schuluniformen haben.

Anna   ____

Sam   I like our school uniform and I like History.

Anna will sagen, dass ihr die Schuluniform auch gefällt, aber dass ihr Lieblingsfach nicht Geschichte, sondern Mathe ist.

Anna   ____

____

Sam   Oh, that's good. You can help me with Maths then.

English G 21

Klassenarbeitstrainer
für Schülerinnen und Schüler

Lösungen und Lerntipps

LISTENING

🎧 01 **Hi!**

Jessica Hi! My name is Jessica. I'm from Bristol. I'm eleven years old. My favourite colour is black.
My school bag isn't black. It's pink. My favourite day of the week is Friday.

Luke Hi! My name is Luke. I'm from Bristol too. Jessica is my twin sister. My favourite colour is blue.
My school bag isn't blue. It's black. My favourite day of the week is Saturday.

David Hi! My name is David. I'm not from Bristol. I'm from London. I'm twelve.
My favourite colour is green. My school bag is green too. My favourite day of the week is Thursday.

1 Where are they from?

Jessica is from <u>Bristol</u>. Luke is from <u>Bristol</u>. David is from <u>London</u>.

2 How old are they?

Jessica is <u>eleven</u>. Luke is <u>eleven</u>. David is <u>twelve</u>.

3 Jessica, Luke and David

Name	Jessica	Luke	David
Their favourite colour?	black	blue	green
The colour of their school bag?	pink	black	green
Their favourite day?	Friday	Saturday	Thursday

Lerntipp So kannst du **Listening Skills** gut üben:

- Unterstreiche im Hörtext Stellen, die du nicht so gut verstanden hast.
- Höre dir den Text auf der CD noch einmal an und lies dabei laut mit.

LANGUAGE

1 WORDS Luke's calendar

Monday	<u>Thursday</u>
football training	*5:45 Doctor Brown*
<u>Tuesday</u>	<u>Friday</u>
shopping with Mum	*party*
<u>Wednesday</u>	<u>Satur</u>day / Sunday
help Dad	*Weekend!!!*

| **Lerntipp** | Lege dir ein Lernheft an.
Schreibe in dein Lernheft alle **Wochentage**. Unterscheide Wochentage, die ähnlich wie im Deutschen geschrieben werden und Wochentage, die anders sind. |

| **Wochentage**
Ähnlich wie im Deutschen:
Monday – Montag
… | **Wochentage**
Anders als im Deutschen:
Tuesday – Dienstag
… |

2   WORDS What's the time?

1 B; 2 E; 3 A; 4 D; 5 F; 6 C

3   GRAMMAR You and the kids in your school book

1   This is Ananda Kapoor. She's eleven years old. She's from Bristol.

2   This is Jack Hanson. He's eleven years old. He's from Bristol.

3   This is Sophie Carter-Brown. She's eleven years old. She's new in Bristol.

4   This is Dan Shaw with his twin brother Jo. They're twins. They're from Bristol.

5   My name is ____. I'm ____ years old. I'm from ____.

| **Lerntipp** | Du hast in dieser Übung mit **Personalpronomen** gearbeitet.
Die folgende Tabelle gibt dir einen Überblick. Übertrage die Tabelle in dein Lernheft. |

	Personalpronomen (personal pronouns)	
	Singular	**Plural**
1. Person	I'm nice.	We're from Germany.
2. Person	You're nice too.	You're from England.
3. Person	He's a boy. She's a girl. It's a house.	They're from India.

4   GRAMMAR Dan and you

1 *You*   What's your name?   *Dan*   My name is Dan Shaw.

2 *You*   How old are you?   *Dan*   I'm twelve.

3 *You*   Where are you from?   *Dan*   I'm from Bristol.

4 *You*   What's your favourite colour? *Dan*   My favourite colour is blue.

5 *You*   What colour is your pencil case? *Dan*   My pencil case is blue.

| **Lerntipp** | Sammle Fragen aus deinem Buch. Ordne sie nach **Fragen mit Fragewort** und **Fragen ohne Fragewort**. Schreibe sie in dein Lernheft. |

| **Fragen mit Fragewort**
What's your name?
How …
Who …
… | **Fragen ohne Fragewort**
Are the days right?
Is …
Can …
… |

5 WORDS Late for school

1 *Jack* <u>Excuse me</u>, what's the time, please?

  Mrs Schmidt It's ten to nine.

  Jack Thank you, Mrs Schmidt.

  Mrs Schmidt <u>You're welcome</u>.

2 *Jack* I think we're in room 14 now.

  Dan Yes, <u>that's right</u>.

  Jack I'm late.

  Dan <u>Me too</u>.

3 *Mr Kingsley* It's ten past nine. Jack, Dan. You're late!

  Jack and Dan <u>Sorry</u>, sir.

| **Lerntipp** | So kannst du üben. Wähle aus, was du machen möchtest. |

  ☐ Ich lerne diesen Dialog auswendig.
  ☐ Ich schreibe den Dialog in mein Lernheft.

WRITING

Who am I?

Hi,

My name is ___. I'm ten / eleven / twelve (years old). I'm from ___. ___ is in Germany. It's a great place.

My favourite colour is blue / red / white / … My school bag is blue and my pencil case is blue too.

My favourite day is Friday / Saturday / Sunday / … (I can go shopping on Saturday. / No school on Saturday!)

| **Lerntipp** | So kannst du **Writing Skills** gut üben. Wähle aus, was du machen möchtest. |

  ☐ Ich schreibe den Musterlösungstext in mein Lernheft.
  ☐ Ich lerne den Musterlösungstext auswendig.
  ☐ Ich schreibe über ein Kind (Sophie / Jack / …) im Englischbuch.
  ☐ Ich schreibe über meine Freundin / meinen Freund.

READING

Jessica and Luke's shopping list

1   Right – Wrong – Not in the text

Right: 1, 5   Wrong: 3   Not in the text: 2, 4

2   Is it on Mrs Summer's shopping list? Yes *or* No?

No: school bag, two pens, ruler, four exercise books, one glue stick

Yes: pencil case, one pen, nine exercise books, two glue sticks, pencils

> **Lerntipp**   So kannst du **Reading Skills** gut üben:
>
> Lies Text <u>5 Welcome to Hamilton Street</u> im Englischbuch, S. 12.
> Mache zu diesem Text eine Einkaufsliste für Dan und Jo.
> Lies Text <u>6 My favourite colour</u> im Englischbuch, S. 13.
> Schreibe zu diesem Text auf, was Dan und Jo gekauft haben.

LANGUAGE

1   WORDS   Five pencils – five colours

1 <u>white</u>   2 <u>yellow</u>   3 <u>red</u>   4 <u>purple</u>   5 <u>brown</u>

2   WORDS   Luke

1 I'm not a <u>girl</u>. I'm a <u>boy</u>, of course.

2 My school bag isn't <u>new</u>. It's <u>old</u>.

3 My school bag is <u>empty</u>. It isn't <u>full</u>.

4 You can <u>open</u> my school bag, and I can <u>close</u> it.

5 I can't <u>pull</u> this box, but I can <u>push</u> it.

> **Lerntipp**   Schreibe diese Wortpaare in dein Lernheft und sammle weitere Wortpaare.
> Reserviere dafür eine Seite.

3   WORDS   Twins in Form 7JM

1 *Sophie*   Hi, <u>my</u> name is Sophie Carter-Brown. What's <u>your</u> name?

 Jessica   Jessica. Jessica Summer and that's my twin brother. <u>His</u> name is Luke.

2 *Sophie*   Who is <u>your</u> English teacher?

 Jessica   Mr Morton. He is <u>our</u> form teacher too. We are in Form 7JM.

3 *Sophie*   Jo, Dan! Come here. That's Jessica and that's <u>her</u> brother, Luke. They're twins too.

   <u>Their</u> English teacher is Mr Morton. They're in Form 7JM.

 Jo   Hi Jessica! Hi Luke! You're the twins in 7JM and we are the twins in Form 7PK. That's <u>our</u> form!

4 *Jessica*   Who's Dan and who's Jo?

 Jo   I'm Jo and this is Dan. I'm <u>his</u> twin brother and he's <u>my</u> twin brother.

4 SOUNDS Dan's trick with words

1 <u>teacher</u>   2 <u>you</u>   3 <u>good</u>   4 <u>here</u>   5 <u>day</u>

5 WORDS We are late!

1 *Mr Summer*   Oh no! It's <u>seven forty</u> / <u>twenty to eight</u>. I'm late for work.

2 *Jessica*   Oh no! It's <u>nine o'clock</u>. I'm late for school.

3 *Luke*   Oh no! It's <u>five fifty</u> / <u>ten to six</u>. I'm late for football.

4 *Grandma*   Oh no! It's <u>three thirteen</u> / <u>thirteen past three</u>. I'm late for my TV show.

5 *Mrs Summer*   Oh no! It's <u>half past eight</u>. I'm late for the party.

6 WORDS How old are they?

1 Charlie is *five*.

2 Mia and Sue are <u>fifteen</u>.

3 Mr Scott is <u>fifty-five</u>.

4 Mrs Scott is <u>forty-seven</u>.

5 Her car is <u>fourteen</u> years old.

6 Emma is <u>four</u>.

7 Her brother Jacob is <u>thirteen</u>.

8 Mary is <u>thirty-four</u>.

9 Grandpa Scott is <u>eighty</u>.

10 Our cat is <u>eight</u>.

11 And our house is <u>a hundred</u> years old.

WRITING

The things in my school bag

Mögliche Lösung:

In my school bag I've got a purple pencil case, a yellow and a pink exercise book and a blue Maths book. I've got a blue rubber, a yellow glue stick, a red pen and a green pencil in my pencil case.

Lerntipp	So kannst du **Writing Skills** gut üben:
	Mache eine Liste von den Dingen in deiner Schultasche.
	Schreibe eine Geschichte zur Mindmap im Schülerbuch S.12.

READING

Jo's e-mail to his mum

1 This is what Jo likes

Yes: 1, 3, 5   No: 2, 4

2 Right – Wrong – Not in the text

Right: 1, 4, 6, 8, 9   Wrong: 5, 10   Not in the text: 2, 3, 7

> **Lerntipp** So kannst du **Reading Skills** gut üben:
>
> ☐ Lies den Reading-Text noch einmal.
> ☐ Unterstreiche, was du nicht richtig verstanden hast.
> ☐ Lies Text <u>6 Meet Mr Kingsley</u> im Englischbuch, S. 22.

LANGUAGE

1 GRAMMAR New friends

1 *Luke* Hi, I<u>'m</u> / <u>am</u> Luke and who <u>are</u> you?

2 *Dan* <u>I'm</u> / <u>I am</u> Dan. This is Jo. <u>He's</u> / <u>He is</u> my brother.

3 *Luke* <u>Are</u> you twins?

   Dan Yes, we are.

4 *Jo* Where are Sophie and Ananda?

5 *Dan* <u>They're</u> / <u>They are</u> in Dilip's classroom.

6 *Luke* Who <u>are</u> Sophie and Ananda?

7 *Jo* <u>They're</u> / <u>They are</u> my friends.

   Luke And who is Dilip?

8 *Dan* <u>He's</u> / <u>He is</u> Ananda's brother.

9 *Luke* Where is your classroom?

10 *Jo* <u>It's</u> / <u>It is</u> here.

> **Lerntipp** So kannst du üben:
>
> ☐ Unterstreiche in der Musterlösung die Stelle, die für dich ein Problem war.
> ☐ Schreibe den Problemsatz in dein Lernheft.
> ☐ Lies im Englischbuch die Grammar File 2 a.
>   Dort findest du die **Langformen** und die **Kurzformen** vom Verb **(to) be**.
> ☐ Übertrage die Tabelle GF 2 a in dein Lernheft.

2 GRAMMAR Short answers

1	Is Mr Kingsley a teacher?	Yes, <u>he is</u>.
2	Are Dan and Jo twins?	Yes, <u>they are</u>.
3	Has Jack got a parrot?	Yes, <u>he has</u>.
4	Has he got a brother?	No, <u>he hasn't</u>.
5	Can Polly swim?	No, <u>she can't</u>.
6	Can Polly say 'Good morning'?	Yes, <u>she can</u>.
7	Is Toby a dog?	No, <u>he isn't</u>.
8	Is he Sophie's brother?	Yes, <u>he is</u>.
9	Are you ten?	<u>Yes, I am.</u> / <u>No, I'm not.</u>
10	Can you sing?	<u>Yes, I can.</u> / <u>No, I can't.</u>

Lerntipp So kannst du üben:

- Unterstreiche in der Musterlösung die Stelle, die für dich ein Problem war.
- Schreibe den Problemsatz in dein Lernheft.
- Lies im Englischbuch die Grammar File 2 c.
  Dort findest du die **Kurzantworten** zum Verb **(to) be**.
- Lies im Englischbuch die Grammar File 3 c.
  Dort findest du die **Kurzantworten** zu **can**.
- Lies im Englischbuch die Grammar File 5 c.
  Dort findest du die **Kurzantworten** zu **have got**.

---

3 GRAMMAR What have they got? What haven't they got?

1 *Has* Sophie got a ruler? Yes, she <u>has</u>. But she hasn't got <u>a rubber</u>.

2 *Have* Jessica and Luke <u>got</u> felt tips? Yes, they <u>have</u>. But <u>they haven't got pencils</u>.

3 <u>Has</u> Mr Hanson got a timetable? No, he <u>hasn't</u>. But <u>he has</u> / <u>he's got a calendar</u>.

4 <u>Have</u> Jo and Dan <u>got</u> an MP3 player? Yes, <u>they have</u>. But <u>they haven't got a mobile phone</u>.

5 <u>Has Ananda got</u> a banana? Yes, she <u>has</u>. But <u>she hasn't got an apple</u>.

4 GRAMMAR Do this! Don't do that!

1 <u>Tell</u> me your names, please.

2 Jack, <u>give</u> me your pencil, please, but <u>don't throw</u> it.

3 Now, <u>take out</u> your English books and <u>open</u> your books at page 29.

4 <u>Look</u> at the picture and <u>do</u> exercise 10.

5 Dan and Jo, <u>don't talk</u>! <u>Listen</u> to me, please.

6 Ananda, <u>read</u> sentence 1, please.

5 PRONUNCIATION 'a' *or* 'an'?

a <u>red ruler</u>, a <u>uniform</u>, a <u>yellow pen</u>, a <u>new word</u>, a <u>joke</u>

an <u>exercise book</u>, an <u>idea</u>, an <u>empty bag</u>, an <u>apple</u>, an <u>art lesson</u>

WRITING

Hi Mum

Hi Mum,

It is Jo's turn in the kitchen today and I can write to you about school and everything now. Our new school is OK. (It's a big school.) There are 30 students in our form and I've got lots of new friends. I like the new school uniform. (It's blue and blue is my favourite colour.) (We've got lots of different subjects.) My favourite subjects are PE and Geography. Our Geography teacher is great. (His name is Mr Barker.) He has got a book about New Zealand. I think New Zealand is great, but a mum in New Zealand isn't great.

Love, Dan

▸ *Die Ideen in Klammern zeigen dir, wie du deinen Brief ausbauen kannst.*

Lerntipp	So kannst du **Writing Skills** gut üben:

Unterstreiche in der Musterlösung Sätze, die du dir merken möchtest.

Schreibe den Musterlösungstext in dein Lernheft.

Lerne den Musterlösungstext auswendig.

LISTENING

🎧 04 **Lunch break at school**

	Sarah	Hi Sam. How's your first day at school?
	Sam	It's OK. But my timetable isn't OK.
	Sarah	Why? What's wrong with your timetable?
	Sam	Our first lesson is Maths on Monday, Maths on Tuesday, Maths on Wednesday and Maths on Friday.
5	*Sarah*	And who is your Maths teacher?
	Sam	It's Mr Hamilton again. He's our form teacher too.
	Sarah	Oh no! Poor Sam. Maths on Monday, Tuesday, Wednesday and Friday. So what is your first lesson on Thursday?
	Sam	Let me see. The first lesson on Thursday is Science.
10	*Sarah*	And who is your Science teacher?
	Sam	Mrs Cooper.
	Sarah	Mrs Cooper?
	Sam	Yes. Mrs Cooper. She's new here. She's from India.
	Sarah	What's your lesson after lunch break today?
15	*Sam*	History.
	Sarah	History. Your favourite subject. And who's your History teacher?
	Sam	Miss Smith.
	Sarah	Oh, Miss Smith. Your favourite teacher!
	Sam	Yes, she's a great teacher.
20	*Sarah*	What about your classmates?
	Sam	There's a new girl. Her name is Anna Schnitzer.
	Sarah	Anna Schnitzer?
	Sam	She's from Germany and she's nice.
	Sarah	And you like her a lot. Anna Schnitzer from Germany and Sam Evans from Bristol.
25	*Sam*	Don't laugh, Sarah!
	Sarah	Sorry, Sam.
	Sam	It's 1.35. I've got History now.
	Sarah	Good luck with Miss Smith and Anna Schnitzer.
	Sam	That's enough, Sarah!
30	*Sarah*	Bye, Sam. See you after school.

1 Sam's timetable

Monday	Tuesday	Wednesday	Thursday	Friday
Maths	Maths	Maths	Science	Maths

2 Sam's teachers and their subjects

Teachers	Form teacher	Maths	Science	History
Mr Hamilton	✔	✔		
Mrs Cooper			✔	
Miss Smith				✔

3 Right or wrong?

Right: 1, 3, 5, 6   Wrong: 2, 4, 7

<table>
<tr><td>Lerntipp</td><td>So kannst du Listening Skills gut üben:</td></tr>
</table>

- Schaue dir den Lerntipp auf S. 2 an.
- Höre dir den Text auf der CD an und lies laut mit.
- Lerne den Dialog auswendig und sprich ihn frei nach.

LANGUAGE

1   GRAMMAR Sarah Evans is in a wheelchair

1 *Sophie*   Are you Sarah Evans? <u>I'm</u> Sophie Carter-Brown.

2 *Sarah*   Yes, <u>I am</u>. <u>I'm</u> / <u>I am</u> new here.

3 *Sophie*   <u>Is</u> your timetable OK?

4 *Sarah*   Well, <u>it's</u> / <u>it is</u> OK, but I can't do sports at school.

5 *Sophie*   <u>Are</u> the kids in your form nice?

6 *Sarah*   Yes, <u>they are</u>. Our teachers are nice too.

7 *Sophie*   <u>Is</u> Mr Kingsley your English teacher?

8 *Sarah*   No, <u>he isn't</u>. Miss Taylor is our English teacher and <u>she's</u> / <u>she</u> is our form teacher too.

<table>
<tr><td>Lerntipp</td><td>Das Verb (to) be: Kurzformen und Langformen
Übertrage die Tabelle in dein Lernheft.</td></tr>
</table>

Kurzformen	**Langformen**
I**'m** eleven.	I **am** eleven.
You**'re** twelve.	You **are** twelve.
He**'s** thirteen.	He **is** thirteen.
She**'s** fourteen.	She **is** fourteen.
It**'s** old.	It **is** old.
We**'re** fifteen.	We **are** fifteen.
You**'re** sixteen.	You **are** sixteen.
They**'re** seventeen.	They **are** seventeen.

2   GRAMMAR Questions for you

1 *Sophie*   Are you from Germany?   *You*   Yes, <u>I am</u>.

2 *Jo*   Are your friends from Germany too?   *You*   Yes, <u>they are</u>.

3 *Dan*   Are you and your friends in Form 7?   *You*   No, <u>we aren't</u>.

4 *Jack*   Is your English teacher nice?   *You*   <u>Yes, he / she is.</u> / <u>No, he / she isn't.</u>

5 *Dilip*   Is your school a big school?   *You*   <u>Yes it is.</u> / <u>No it isn't.</u>

<table>
<tr><td rowspan="2">Lerntipp</td><td>Kurzantworten</td></tr>
<tr><td>Im Deutschen antworten wir oft noch kürzer mit Ja oder Nein. Aber das ist im Englischen unhöflich. Mit der Tabelle kannst du die höfliche englische Form üben:
Decke die 2. und die 3. Spalte ab und lies die Fragen.
Sage zu jeder Frage eine Kurzantwort mit Yes, … und eine Kurzantwort mit No, …
Überprüfe deine Kurzantworten. Decke dazu die 2. und 3. Spalte auf.</td></tr>
</table>

Frage	Kurzantwort **bejaht** Verwende immer die **Langform**	Kurzantwort **verneint** Verwende die **Kurzform**
Are you eleven?	Yes, I **am**.	No, I**'m not**.
Is your friend eleven?	Yes, he **is**. / Yes, she **is**.	No, he **isn't**. / No, she **isn't**.
Is your house old?	Yes, it **is**.	No, it **isn't**.
Are you and David friends?	Yes, we **are**.	No, we **aren't**.
Are we your friends?	Yes, you **are**.	No, you **aren't**.
Are your friends eleven?	Yes, they **are**.	No, they **aren't**.

3 GRAMMAR / WORDS What's there in Sam's room? What isn't there?

1 <u>There is / There's</u> a table, but <u>there isn't</u> a chair.

2 <u>There is / There's</u> a computer on his desk and <u>there are</u> books on the floor.

3 <u>Is there</u> a football under his bed? – No, <u>there isn't</u>.

4 <u>Are there</u> comics on his bed? – Yes, <u>there are</u>.

5 <u>Are there</u> posters on the wall? – No, <u>there aren't</u>.

4 GRAMMAR What have you got?

1 I've got <u>a dog</u>, but I haven't got <u>a cat</u> and I haven't got <u>a parrot</u>. *(mögliche Lösung)*

2 I<u>'ve got a skateboard and a football</u>, but <u>I haven't got a boat</u> and I haven't got <u>a kite</u>. *(mögliche Lösung)*

3 I<u>'ve got a chair</u>, but <u>I haven't got a wheelchair</u>. *(mögliche Lösung)*

4 I<u>'ve got a calendar</u>, but <u>I haven't got a newspaper</u>. *(mögliche Lösung)*

5 I<u>'ve got a school bag</u>, but <u>I haven't got a box</u>. *(mögliche Lösung)*

5 GRAMMAR Do this! Don't do that!

1 *Sarah*   Don't throw your things on my table and <u>don't play</u> football with my school bag!

2 *Mrs Evans*   Hurry up, Sam and <u>take</u> this box to Mrs Kapoor, but <u>don't drop</u> it.

3 *Mrs Kapoor*   Come in, Sam. <u>Meet</u> my friend Dinaz. She's from India.

4 *Dinaz*   Hi, Sam. Sit with us and <u>have</u> a cup of tea.

6 WORDS Birthdays

1 *Sarah*   My birthday is on <u>22nd October</u>.

2 *Sam*   My birthday <u>is on 3rd March</u>.

3 *Anna*   My <u>birthday is on 15th December</u>.

4 *Jessica & Luke*   Our <u>birthday is on 31st July</u>.

5 *You*   My <u>birthday is on</u> ___________________________ .

GETTING BY IN ENGLISH

Anna Schnitzer's first day at school

Anna Hi, I'm Anna Schnitzer. I'm new here. I'm from Germany.

Sam Hi, I'm Sam. Welcome to our form.

Anna Excuse me, but I haven't got a chair.

Sam Here you are. An empty chair for you.

Anna Can I sit with you?

Sam Yes, you can.

Anna What have we got next?

Sam It's Maths with Mr Hamilton, then English with Miss Taylor in room 7.
After lunch break there is History in room 11 and then PE.

Anna I can't remember all that.

Sam Here's a timetable for you.

Anna Thank you. German schools are different from English schools.

Sam What's different?

Anna German students haven't got school uniforms.

Sam I like our school uniform and I like History.

Anna I like your school uniform too, but my favourite subject isn't History. It's Maths.

Sam Oh, that's good. You can help me with Maths then.

Lerntipp So kannst du **Getting by in English** gut üben:

- Unterstreiche in der Musterlösung Sätze, die du dir merken möchtest.
- Lies den Musterlösungsdialog einmal laut vor.

READING

A day in the life of Luke Summer

1 Luke's parents

Right: 2, 4, 5, 6   Wrong: 3, 8   Not in the text: 1, 7

2 Luke or Jessica?

Luke: 1, 3, 4, 5, 6, 7   Jessica: 2, 3, 4, 5, 8

3 The restaurant

1 The name of the restaurant is <u>The Summer Place</u>.

2 The restaurant opens at <u>10.30</u>.

3 *Luke* The guests like <u>Dad's food</u>. Dad likes <u>his guests</u>.

> **Lerntipp**   So kannst du **Reading Skills** gut üben:
>
> Lies den Text jemandem laut vor.
> Unterstreiche mit verschiedenen Farbstiften, was zu jeder Person im Text steht.
> Lies nur die Textstellen, die sich auf Lukes Vater und Mutter beziehen.

LANGUAGE

1 GRAMMAR Luke's friends at school

1 I'm in Form 7JM, but <u>my</u> new friends are in Form 7PK.

2 This is Dan and <u>his</u> twin brother Jo.

3 They are nice, and <u>their</u> jokes are great.

4 Jack is <u>my</u> friend too.

5 <u>His</u> dad has got a Bed and Breakfast and a parrot.

6 <u>Its</u> cage is in the kitchen.

7 This is Ananda and <u>her</u> friend Sophie.

8 <u>Their</u> friends are Dan, Jo and Jack too.

9 <u>Our</u> school is a big school.

10 What about you? Is <u>your</u> school big too?

<table>
<tr><td>Lerntipp</td><td colspan="2">Die Tabelle gibt dir einen Überblick über Personalpronomen und Possessivbegleiter.
Übertrage sie in dein Lernheft.</td></tr>
<tr><td></td><td>Personal pronouns</td><td>Possessive determiners</td></tr>
<tr><td>Singular 1. Person
2. Person
3. Person</td><td>I can play football.
You are my friend.
He is from London.
She has got a cat and a dog.
It is very old.</td><td>My brother can play football too.
Your teacher is nice.
His girlfriend is from London too.
Her cat is big.
Its legs (= Beine) are white.</td></tr>
<tr><td>Plural 1. Person
2. Person
3. Person</td><td>We are from Bristol.
You are from Germany.
They are at school now.</td><td>Our flat is above a shop.
Your friends are from Germany too.
Their school is nice.</td></tr>
</table>

2   GRAMMAR / WORDS Who is who in Luke's family?

1   Luke is Jessica's <u>brother</u>.

2   Andrea is Jessica and Luke's <u>cousin</u>.

3   Jessica is Mary and Joe's <u>daughter</u>.

4   Jane Kiefer and Bob Scott are Luke's <u>aunt and uncle</u>.

5   Bob is Grandma and Grandpa Scott's <u>son</u>.

3   WORDS Luke and his family

1   Mary and Joe are my <u>parents</u>. They are married. They are not d<u>ivorced</u>.

2   Emma, Jacob, Jessica and I are Grandma and Grandpa Scott's <u>grandchildren</u>.

3   Grandma Summer and Grandpa Summer are d<u>ead</u>.

4   Emma, Jacob and Andrea are my <u>cousins</u>.

4   GRAMMAR It's the same every day!

1   I <u>have</u> a shower every morning, Luke <u>has</u> a shower every evening.

2   I <u>do</u> my homework in the afternoon, Luke <u>does</u> his homework in the evening.

3   I <u>tidy</u> my room every day, and Luke <u>tidies</u> his room.

4   I <u>go</u> to the rabbit hutch, Luke <u>goes</u> to his friends.

5   I <u>play</u> with my rabbits, Luke <u>plays</u> football with his friends.

<table>
<tr><td>Lerntipp</td><td>Simple present: Die richtige Schreibweise
Bei manchen Verben ändert sich die Schreibweise, wenn man das 3. Person -s anhängt.
Die Tabelle hilft dir, die richtige Schreibweise zu üben.
Übertrage sie in dein Lernheft und finde für jede Spalte weitere Verben.
Weitere Verben findest du in der Grammar File 7 b im Schulbuch.</td></tr>
</table>

Simple present: Meine 3. Person -s Tabelle		
He / She / It -s	**He / She / It -es**	**He / She / It -ies**
pla**ys** fee**ds** …	go**es** wash**es** …	tid**ies** hurr**ies** …

5   GRAMMAR The Summer family

1   Luke <u>doesn't do</u> judo. He <u>plays</u> football.

2   Jessica <u>doesn't play</u> football. She <u>has</u> music lessons.

3   Mr and Mrs Summer <u>don't have</u> time at weekends. They <u>work</u> at the restaurant.

4   *Aunt Jane*   I <u>don't live</u> in England. My family and I <u>live</u> in Germany.

5   Andrea <u>speaks</u> English with her mum, but she <u>doesn't speak</u> English with her dad.

> **Lerntipp** **Simple present – Verneinung: don't** oder **doesn't**
> Schreibe die Sätze der Aufgabe 5 in dein Lernheft. Unterstreiche die Verneinungen.
> Lies die Grammar File 7 c in deinem Schulbuch.

6   WORDS The Summers and their friends

1   Mr Summer's friend isn't married and he doesn't have a girlfriend. He is s<u>ingle</u>.

2   Sam is Luke's friend. His parents aren't together. They are d<u>ivorced</u>.

3   Luke thinks History is boring. But Jessica thinks it is <u>interesting</u>.

4   Mrs Summer's friend doesn't like cold tea. She only likes her tea h<u>ot</u>.

5   German is easy for Mr Kiefer, but he thinks English is d<u>ifficult</u>.

WRITING

A morning in my family

Every morning I get up at seven o'clock. I clean my teeth and wash my face, but I don't have a shower in the morning. Then I get dressed and I get my things ready for school. Sometimes I make my bed. Mum and Dad get up early. Mum feeds our guinea pigs. After that she reads the newspaper and Dad makes breakfast. Then we have breakfast together and I take a sandwich to school. Dad goes to work at 7:30 and he takes me to school in his car. Mum doesn't go to work because she works at home at the computer.

> **Lerntipp** So kannst du **Writing Skills** gut üben:
>
> Unterstreiche die **Satzanfänge** in der Musterlösung und in deinem Text.
> Kreise die Wörter **and**, **but**, **because** in der Musterlösung und in deinem Text ein.
> Schreibe den Musterlösungstext in dein Lernheft.

LISTENING

🎧 07 **In the Scotts' garden**

Andrea	You've got two rabbits, Jacob! Two rabbits <u>and</u> a dog!
Jacob	Two rabbits, a dog <u>and</u> an old cat.
Andrea	That's a lot of pets. Who feeds your pets, Jacob?
Jacob	I feed the rabbits. Dad feeds the cat and Mum feeds the dog.
5 *Andrea*	What about your sister?
Jacob	Emma? Emma doesn't feed the rabbits, the cat or the dog. She plays with the rabbits. She plays with the cat and she plays with the dog. But she doesn't feed them and she doesn't clean the rabbits' hutch.
Andrea	So, what about the hutch? Who cleans the hutch, Jacob?
10 *Jacob*	I sometimes clean the hutch.
Andrea	Sometimes?
Jacob	Well, Dad cleans it every Saturday. And I sometimes help him.
Andrea	Have your rabbits got names?
Jacob	It's *Browny* for the brown rabbit and *Blacky* for the black rabbit.
15 *Andrea*	That's easy. What about your dog? What's its name?
Jacob	*Stella* is not an it. Our dog is a she.
Andrea	*Stella*. That's a nice name. How old is she?
Jacob	She is four months old.
Andrea	Four months.
20 *Jacob*	Yeah. Emma is four years old and our dog is four months old. They run up and down the stairs all the time. They go in my room. They sit on my bed. They eat my books.
Andrea	They eat your books?!
Jacob	Well, *Stella* eats my books and Emma reads my books.
Andrea	Emma reads your books?! Emma is four.
25 *Jacob*	Yes, Emma is four, but she can read. She is clever.
Andrea	I haven't got a brother or a sister.
Jacob	But you've got two hamsters, Andrea.
Andrea	No, I haven't got two hamsters. I've got two guinea pigs. Guinea pigs are OK. I feed them and I play with them. But they aren't like a brother or a sister.

1   What pets have they got?

Andrea: <u>guinea pigs</u>   The Scotts: <u>cat</u>, <u>dog</u>, <u>rabbits</u>

2   Who feeds these pets?

Andrea: <u>guinea pigs</u>   Jacob: <u>rabbits</u>   Mrs Scott: <u>dog</u>   Mr Scott: <u>cat</u>

3   Right or wrong?

Right: 2, 3, 5, 7   Wrong: 1, 4, 6

> **Lerntipp**   So kannst du **Listening Skills** gut üben:
>
> - Höre dir den Text auf der CD an und drücke nach jedem Sprecher die Pausentaste. Wiederhole, was der Sprecher gesagt hat.
> - Höre dir den Text auf der CD an und lies dabei den abgedruckten Hörtext mit.
> - Markiere im abgedruckten Hörtext die Stellen, die du anfangs nicht richtig verstanden hast.

LANGUAGE

1   GRAMMAR The Scott family

1   In the morning Mr Scott <u>gets up</u> early and <u>reads</u> the newspaper.

2   Mrs Scott <u>doesn't read</u> the newspaper. She <u>makes</u> breakfast.

3   Jacob and Emma <u>get up</u> after their parents. They <u>don't make</u> breakfast.

4   After breakfast Mr Scott <u>tidies</u> the kitchen before he <u>goes</u> to work.

5   Mrs Scott <u>doesn't tidy</u> the kitchen. She <u>takes</u> Emma to kindergarden.

> **Lerntipp**   **Simple present**
> Lies in deinem Schulbuch die Grammar File 7 a / 7 b und 7 c.
> Mache die drei ‚Polly'-Aufgaben zur Grammar File 7 a und 7 c.

2   GRAMMAR A letter from Andrea

Hi Jacob,

1   How is <u>your</u> new school? <u>My</u> school is OK.

2   We've got two new guinea pigs. <u>Their</u> cage is in <u>our</u> living room.

3   And I've got a rabbit. <u>My</u> rabbit's name is *Pearl*. <u>Her</u> hutch is in the garden.

4   Mum likes <u>her</u> garden, Dad likes <u>his</u> car and I like <u>my</u> pets.

5   What about <u>your</u> pets?

> **Lerntipp**   So kannst du **Possessivbegleiter** und Kurzformen von **(to) be** unterscheiden lernen:
>
> - Mache die ‚Polly'-Aufgabe zur Grammar File 8 im Schülerbuch.
> - Lies die Mustersätze laut vor.
> - Lasse dir die Mustersätze diktieren.
>
> Mustersätze:
> 1   **You're** in **your** garden with **your** dog.
> 2   **He's** in the kitchen with **his** pets.
> 3   **It's** a hamster. **Its** cage is big.
> 4   There are lots of mice. **They're** in a cage, but **their** cage is too small.

3   GRAMMAR Mrs Kiefer and Mrs Scott

1 *Mrs Kiefer*   I <u>get up</u> at 6 o'clock every morning.

   Mrs Scott   I <u>don't get up</u> so early.

2 *Mrs Kiefer*   Herbert <u>has</u> coffee for breakfast, but I <u>have</u> tea.

   Mrs Scott   Bob <u>doesn't like</u> coffee, but I <u>like</u> it.

3 *Mrs Kiefer*   Herbert <u>takes</u> Andrea to school. School <u>starts</u> at 8 o'clock.

   Mrs Scott   Bob <u>doesn't take</u> Jacob to school. School <u>doesn't start</u> at 8 o'clock.

Lerntipp   So kannst du die **Verneinung** im **simple present** üben:

- Markiere bei den Lösungen zu Aufgabe 3 die Verneinungen.
- Schreibe die Tabelle in dein Lernheft und suche im Buch weitere Beispielsätze.

Verneinungen im **simple present**	
doesn't + <u>Verb im Infinitiv</u>	**don't** + <u>Verb im Infinitiv</u>
He **doesn't** <u>do</u> judo. …	You **don't** <u>like</u> me. …

4   GRAMMAR Jacob and Andrea

1 *Andrea*   Where are your rabbits? Are they in a hutch?

   Jacob   Yes, the rabbit<u>s'</u> hutch is in the garden, but the dog<u>'s</u> basket is in the house.

2 *Andrea*   Is this Emma<u>'s</u> room?

   Jacob   No, it isn't. It's Mum and Dad<u>'s</u> room.

3 *Andrea*   Your desk is very old.

   Jacob   It is Grandpa Scott<u>'s</u> desk.

Lerntipp   So kannst du üben, wann man beim **s-Genitiv 's** oder **s'** schreibt:

- Korrigiere deine Fehler und lasse dir Übung 4 diktieren.
- Mache die ‚Polly'-Aufgabe zur Grammar File 9 im Schülerbuch.
- Schreibe die Tabellen in dein Lernheft und ergänze sie.

Singularformen	Genitivformen -'s
teacher parrot mother Jo aunt	The **teacher's** desk The **parrot's** cage My …

Pluralformen	Genitivformen -s'
teacher**s** parrot**s** parent**s** twin**s** the Brown**s**	The teacher**s'** desk The parrot**s'** cage My …

5 WORDS Food for the cat

1 *Mr Scott*   Jacob, you can feed the cat and I can read my book. Can you give me my glasses, <u>please</u>.

  Jacob   Yes, <u>of course</u>, Dad. <u>Here you are.</u>

2 *Mr Scott*   <u>Thanks</u>, Jacob.

  Jacob   Where is the cat food?

3 *Mr Scott*   <u>Sorry</u>, I can't <u>hear</u> you.

  Jacob   The cat food. Where is it?

4 *Mr Scott*   Oh! I don't <u>remember</u>. I <u>think</u> it is in the cupboard.

  Jacob   There is a tin of <u>meat</u>.

5 *Mr Scott*   That's right. Open it and put it in a <u>bowl</u>.

6 WORDS An afternoon in the garden

1 The Scott family and the Kiefer family are together. The two <u>families</u> are in the garden.

2 Andrea can see a <u>mouse</u> under the tree. There are lots of <u>mice</u> in the garden.

3 There are <u>fish</u> in the pond. One <u>fish</u> is really big.

4 The <u>children</u> are hungry and one <u>child</u> is very hungry.

5 That's Emma. She has got a pizza <u>box</u>. There are more pizza <u>boxes</u> in the kitchen.

Lerntipp So kannst du die Pluralformen üben:
Verbessere deine Fehler paarweise: Singularform – Pluralform.
Mache die ‚Polly'-Aufgabe zur Grammar File 6 im Schülerbuch.
Übertrage die Tabelle in dein Lernheft und ergänze sie.

Besondere Pluralformen		
Plural **-es**	Plural **-ies**	Sonderformen
box box**es**	baby babi**es** …	tooth teeth …

GETTING BY IN ENGLISH

Sundays

Bob Scott   I like Sundays. On Sundays I don't get up early, I don't go to work, I don't sit at my desk. On Sundays there is enough time to be with the family.

Herbert Kiefer   Was sagt er da? Heute ist doch gar nicht Sonntag.

Andrea   Onkel Bob hat gesagt, <u>dass er Sonntage mag und dass er am Sonntag nicht früh aufsteht, nicht zur Arbeit geht und nicht an seinem Schreibtisch sitzt. Am Sonntag gibt es genug Zeit für die Familie.</u>

Herbert Kiefer   Der hat's gut! Sag ihm mal, dass das bei uns anders ist: Papa steht früh auf und sitzt am Schreibtisch. Er arbeitet auch am Sonntag und er macht das Frühstück.

Andrea   Well, Sundays are different for Dad. He <u>gets up early and sits at his desk. He works on Sundays too, and he makes breakfast.</u>

Bob Scott   Well, after breakfast I work in my garden. Sometimes the kids help me in the garden. Jacob feeds the rabbits or climbs the trees and Emma plays in her little garden house.

Herbert Kiefer   Er arbeitet im Garten?

Andrea   Ja, nach dem Frühstück arbeitet er im Garten. <u>Manchmal helfen ihm die Kinder. Jacob füttert die Hasen oder klettert auf die Bäume und Emma spielt in ihrem Gartenhaus.</u>

Bob Scott   Sunday afternoons we go to Grandma and Grandpa's house.

Andrea   Sonntagnachmittag <u>besuchen die Scotts Oma und Opa.</u>

Herbert Kiefer   Und was machen sie am Abend?

Andrea   <u>And what do you do on Sunday evening?</u>

Bob Scott   We sometimes play board games (= Brettspiele) or watch TV together.

Andrea   <u>Sie spielen manchmal Brettspiele oder gucken zusammen fern.</u>

Lerntipp   So kannst du **Getting by in English** gut üben:

- Unterstreiche in der Musterlösung Sätze, die dir bei der Übertragung vom Englischen ins Deutsche schwergefallen sind.
- Unterstreiche in der Musterlösung Sätze, die dir bei der Übertragung vom Deutschen ins Englische schwergefallen sind.
- Übertrage die deutschen Mustersätze wieder ins Englische.

Unit 3 — Lösungen A

LISTENING

🎧 10 Sport and hobbies

Luke	Do kids in Germany play football a lot?
Andrea	Yes, lots of kids play football. Girls play football too.
Luke	Do you play football, Andrea?
Andrea	No, Luke, I don't. But Dad plays football. He loves football. It's his favourite sport and he's in a football club.
Luke	What do you do in your free time, Andrea?
Andrea	I play the guitar and I really like it. But what I really love are horses!
Luke	Horses? So you've got a horse, Andrea?
Andrea	No, Luke, I haven't. But our neighbours have got horses. Horses are a lot of work. You have to feed them and clean the place.
Luke	So you go there and you feed the horses?
Andrea	Yes, I often help Sascha and Monika with the horses.
Luke	Sascha and Monika?
Andrea	They're my friends. They have to help their parents on the farm a lot and I help them. Sascha is really great with horses.
Luke	Sascha is great with horses? How?
Andrea	Well, you know, they never run away when he is with them. He often rides Ambassador, a black horse. He's a scary horse and only Sascha can ride him.
Luke	Are you great with horses too, Andrea?
Andrea	No, I'm not. Monika and I usually ride Pax and Laurette. Pax and Laurette are two old horses. They aren't scary. But now tell me about you, Luke. What do you do in your free time?
Luke	Well, I like sport. American football, baseball, hockey.
Andrea	You play American football, baseball and hockey!?
Luke	No, I don't play sport. I watch it on TV a lot.
Andrea	Oh Luke!

1 What do they do in their free time?

Andrea's dad: plays football; is in a club

Andrea: plays the guitar; rides horses

Luke: watches sport on TV

2 Andrea and her friends

Right: 1, 2, 5, 6   Wrong: 3, 4, 7

3 What does Andrea do on the farm?

Right: A, C, D   Wrong: B, E, F

> **Lerntipp**   So kannst du **Listening Skills** gut üben:
>
> - Höre dir den Text auf der CD an.
> - Notiere dir, wer welche Aktivität macht.
> - Höre dir den Text erneut an und ergänze deine Liste.

LANGUAGE

1   GRAMMAR At a sports club

1 Julian <u>plays badminton</u>, but he <u>doesn't do judo</u>.

2 Esther <u>doesn't play hockey</u>, but she <u>goes swimming</u>.

3 Sven and Britta <u>play hockey</u>, but they <u>don't go swimming</u>.

4 The Devlins <u>don't play badminton</u>, but they <u>do judo</u>.

5 Naomi <u>plays badminton</u>, but she <u>doesn't play hockey</u>.

6 The Browns <u>play hockey</u>, but they <u>don't do judo</u>.

7 And you? I <u>play football / go dancing / ...</u>, but I <u>don't do judo / don't go riding / ...</u>

2   GRAMMAR What sport do they do?

1 <u>Do the Coopers play hockey too?</u>   No, they <u>don't</u>.

2 <u>Does Claudia go riding too?</u>   No, she <u>doesn't</u>.

3 <u>Do his parents play table tennis too?</u>   No, they <u>don't</u>.

4 <u>Do you do sport at school too?</u>   Yes, I <u>do</u>.

> **Lerntipp**   **Simple present – Fragesätze** mit **do / does**

		Aussagesätze	Fragesätze
Singular	1. Person	I play hockey.	**Do** I play hockey?
	2. Person	You play football.	**Do** you play football?
	3. Person	He play**s** tennis.	**Does** he <u>play</u> tennis?
		She play**s** the guitar.	**Does** she <u>play</u> tennis?
		It run**s** away.	**Does** it <u>run</u> away?
Plural	1. Person	We watch matches.	**Do** we watch matches?
	2. Person	You like skating.	**Do** you like skating?
	3. Person	They always win.	**Do** they always win?

3   GRAMMAR How often do you go swimming?

1 <u>When do the Millers play hockey?</u>

2 <u>Where do Anna and Sabrina go riding?</u>

3 <u>Why does Toby play table tennis?</u>

4 <u>How often do Lisa and Toby play table tennis?</u>

Lerntipp	So kannst du üben, **Fragesätze** mit **do**, **does** und <u>Fragewort</u> richtig zu bilden: Lies die **Aussagesätze**. Wähle **Fragewörter** aus und bilde **Fragen** aus den **Aussagesätzen**. Decke dazu die letzte Spalte zu. Achte besonders auf die **3. Person Singular**. Überprüfe, ob deine Fragesätze richtig sind.

		Aussagesätze	**Frage-wörter**	**Fragesätze**
Singular	1. Person	I play hockey.	What	<u>What</u> do I do at the weekend?
	2. Person	You go dancing.	Where	<u>Where</u> **do** you go dancing?
	3. Person	He do**es** judo.	When	<u>When</u> **does** he <u>do</u> judo?
		She play**s** the guitar.	When	<u>When</u> **does** she <u>play</u> the guitar?
		It run**s** away.	Why	<u>Why</u> **does** it <u>run</u> away?
Plural	1. Person	We watch the match.	When	<u>When</u> **do** we watch the match?
	2. Person	You like skating.	Why	<u>Why</u> **do** you like skating?
	3. Person	They always win.	Why	<u>Why</u> **do** they always win?

4   GRAMMAR Who has to feed the horses?

1 *Anna*   I <u>have to feed</u> the horses, but I <u>don't have to clean</u> their boxes.

2 *Sabrina*   No, Anna. You <u>have to clean</u> the boxes but you <u>don't have to feed</u> the horses.

3 *Mr Rider* We all <u>have to clean</u> the boxes and we <u>have to feed</u> the horses.

4 *Mr Rider* Ted <u>has to take</u> the horses back to the box, the girls <u>don't have to do</u> that.

5 *Mr Rider* They <u>have to make</u> sandwiches, Ted can help them, but he <u>doesn't have to help</u>.

Lerntipp	So kannst du üben, **(to) have to** richtig zu verwenden: Lies die **Aussagesätze** und bilde **verneinte Sätze**. Decke dazu die dritte Spalte ab.

		Aussagesätze	**Verneinte Sätze**
Singular	1. Person	I **have to** buy food	I <u>don't</u> **have to** buy food
	2. Person	You **have to** get up.	You <u>don't</u> **have to** get up.
	3. Person	He **has to** lay the table.	He <u>doesn't</u> **have to** lay the table.
		She **has to** call the police.	She <u>doesn't</u> **have to** call the police.
		It **has to** fit.	It <u>doesn't</u> **have to** fit.
Plural	1. Person	We **have to** start now.	We <u>don't</u> **have to** start now.
	2. Person	You **have to** collect cards.	You <u>don't</u> **have to** collect cards.
	3. Person	They **have to** do sport.	They <u>don't</u> **have to** do sport.

5   GRAMMAR Prunella and Uncle Henry

		Adverbs
1	✔ Prunella ✔ plays tennis with uncle Henry.	(sometimes)
2	✔ They ✔ play with rackets.	(usually)
3	Uncle Henry doesn't have a head, so Prunella ✔ wins.	(always)
4	The neighbours ✔ call the police.	(never)
5	But they ✔ shout at them because of the noise.	(often)

Lerntipp	So kannst du üben, **Häufigkeitsadverbien** richtig zu verwenden: Häufigkeitsadverbien stehen im **simple present** gewöhnlich <u>vor dem Vollverb</u>. Es ist also wichtig, dass du in jedem Satz das Vollverb finden kannst.

- Decke die 3. Spalte ab.
- Unterstreiche in den Sätzen der 1. Spalte das Vollverb.
- Füge jetzt die Häufigkeitsadverbien der 2. Spalte ein.
- Überprüfe anhand der 3. Spalte, ob deine Sätze richtig sind.

	Häufigkeits-adverbien	
1 Mr Smith gets up early.	always	1 Mr Smith **always** <u>gets</u> up early.
2 He doesn't go to work before nine.	usually	2 He doesn't **usually** <u>go</u> to work before nine.*
3 He plays tennis in the morning.	often	3 He **often** <u>plays</u> tennis in the morning.
4 He doesn't always win.	always	4 He doesn't **always** <u>win</u>.
5 After tennis he has a second breakfast.	sometimes	5 After tennis he **sometimes** <u>has</u> a second breakfast.
		* richtig ist hier auch: He **usually** doesn't <u>go</u> to work before nine.

6   STUDY SKILLS Make a dictionary

se – sh	<u>se</u>ll, <u>sh</u>are, <u>sh</u>irt, <u>sh</u>oe, <u>sh</u>op
si – sk	<u>si</u>ng, <u>si</u>ngle, <u>si</u>nk, <u>si</u>ze, <u>sk</u>ate

GETTING BY IN ENGLISH

Hi Jack,

In my free time I play computer games. I always play in the evenings after my homework. Mum doesn't like it. She never plays computer games, but Dad sometimes plays with me at the weekend. My favourite sport is football. I play football in a football club on Wednesday and on Saturday. We usually have matches on Saturday. We are a good team and we have a lot of fun, but we don't always win of course. Dad likes football too, but he doesn't play football. We often watch football matches together on TV.

What do you do in your free time? What do you do after school and what is your favourite sport?

Love, Adrian

Lerntipp	So kannst du **Getting by in English** gut üben:

- Unterstreiche in der Lösung die Häufigkeitsadverbien: **always, never, sometimes, usually, often**
- Unterstreiche in deinem Brief die Häufigkeitsadverbien:
  always, never, sometimes, usually, often
- Schreibe die Fragen an Jack in dein Lernheft.

READING

What I do in my free time

1 Sarah

Right: 1, 2, 4, 5   Wrong: 6, 7, 8   Not in the text: 3, 9, 10

2 Sarah's mum

1 Sarah's mum works in a shop.

2 She usually works till eight o'clock in the evening.

3 But on Tuesdays and Fridays she is home at five o'clock.

4 She eats a sandwich before they go to Sarah's training.

3 Sarah and basketball

1 b; 2 a und c; 3 c; 4 b

Lerntipp   So kannst du **Reading Skills** gut üben:

- Lies den Reading-Text noch einmal.
- Schreibe in dein Lernheft, was du über Sarah weißt.
- Schreibe in dein Lernheft, was du über Sarahs Basketball-Team weißt.
- Schreibe in dein Lernheft, was du über Sarahs Mutter weißt.

LANGUAGE

1 GRAMMAR At the shop

1 *Mr Cox*   Where do you put the T-shirts Mrs Turner?

2 *Mr Cox*   When does Miss Broom clean the shelves?

3 *Mr Cox*   What does Mr Cheap do?

4 *Mr Cox*   How often do you sell dresses?

5 *Mr Cox*   Why do we have a lot of dresses then?

Lerntipp   Du willst üben, wie du Fragesätze mit **Fragewort** und **(to) do** bildest?
Lies dazu den Lerntipp auf der Seite 24 im Lösungsheft.

2   GRAMMAR The Turners at home

1   Mum and Dad have to go to work.

2   Tina has to go to school and (she has to) clean the cage.

3   Dad has to go shopping.

4   Tina and Dad have to feed the hamsters.

5   Mum has to make dinner.

3   GRAMMAR What don't they have to do?

1   Tina doesn't have to go to work and she doesn't have to go shopping / doesn't have to make dinner.

2   Mum and Dad don't have to go to school and they don't have to clean the cage.

3   Mum doesn't have to clean the cage and she doesn't have to feed the hamsters.

4   Dad doesn't have to go to school and he doesn't have to clean the cage.

5   Tina and Dad don't have to make dinner.

4   GRAMMAR The Carter-Browns – what do they have to do?

1   Does Toby have to feed the pets?   Yes, he does.

2   Do Dad and Sophie have to clean the bathroom?   No, they don't.

3   Does Mum have to wash the car?   No, she doesn't.

4   Do Emily, Sophie and Toby have to go to work?   No, they don't.

5   *Sophie*   Do you have to help your mum in the kitchen?   Yes, I do. / No, I don't.

> **Lerntipp**   Du willst üben, **(to) have to** richtig zu verwenden?
> Lies den Lerntipp auf S. 24 im Lösungsheft.

5   GRAMMAR Poor Sophie

1   I always have to help Mum in the kitchen.

2   Toby never has to help Mum in the kitchen.

3   He can often play in his room or in the garden. / He often can play …

4   Emily sometimes goes shopping with Mum. / Sometimes Emily goes shopping with Mum.

5   Emily usually comes home with new clothes.

> **Lerntipp**   Häufigkeitsadverbien
>
> **always** – immer, **often** – oft, **usually** – normalerweise, gewöhnlich, meistens,
> **never** – nie, **sometimes** – manchmal
>
> Sammle aus deinem Schülerbuch und dem Workbook Sätze mit Häufigkeitsadverbien.
> Schreibe sie in dein Lernheft. Unterstreiche in diesen Sätzen die Häufigkeitsadverbien.
>
> Beispiel
> I never go to football matches.

WRITING

This is Brian's life:

At home he has to help his mum <u>in the kitchen</u>. <u>He has to lay the table, but he doesn't have to clean the kitchen.</u> He can play the piano. / He has to play the piano <u>every day</u>. <u>And</u> he collects stamps. <u>It's his favourite hobby.</u> At school he has to listen to his teachers, <u>answer their questions and do what they say</u>. And he has to write <u>lots of</u> tests. <u>But</u> he can do sports. He can play basketball <u>in a team or do judo</u>. He often phones his friends. They sometimes meet <u>in the afternoons</u>. They play football <u>or computer games</u>, but they never go shopping, <u>because Brian hates shopping</u>.

Lerntipp | Interessant schreiben können

Natürlich erfüllst du die Aufgabe auch, wenn du zu jeder Idee in der Mindmap nur einen Satz schreibst und die Sätze einfach aneinander reihst.
Die unterstrichenen Sätze im Lösungsvorschlag zeigen dir, wie man **Ideen ausbauen** kann und die **Sätze miteinander verknüpfen** kann.

Und so kann ich üben, interessante Texte zu schreiben:
- Ich lese den Musterlösungstext <u>mit</u> allen unterstrichenen Teilen.
- Ich lese den Musterlösungstext <u>ohne</u> die unterstrichenen Teile.
- Ich ergänze in meinem Text weitere Ideen.
- Ich verknüpfe in meinem Text Ideen mit **and**, **but**, **because** und **or**.

LISTENING

🎧 13 **An invitation list**

Luke	Jessica, what are you doing here in my room on my computer?
Jessica	I'm making a list.
Luke	A list?
Jessica	It's our birthday next week. We can have a party and we can invite twelve friends.
5 *Luke*	Twelve friends on our twelfth birthday.
Jessica	That's right. So we need an invitation list for our birthday party and I'm writing down the names of all my friends.
Luke	All *your* friends? What about *my* friends?
Jessica	You can invite some friends too.
10 *Luke*	I want to invite the SHoCK Team.
Jessica	The Shock team? You mean the five mad kids in Form 7PK?
Luke	They aren't mad, Jessica. They're great and they are my friends.
Jessica	Listen Luke, I don't want to put their names on the invitation list and I don't want to make invitation cards for them.
15 *Luke*	You don't have to. I can write them an e-mail. You can make your list and give invitation cards to your friends.
Jessica	Oh Luke. Let's not argue. Let's have a really nice party.
Luke	A really nice party with really nice people.
Jessica	Yes, and really nice games.
20 *Luke*	And lots of food. My friends are always hungry and thirsty. Pizza, chicken legs and cheese for the SHoCK Team.
Jessica	Chocolate cake and ice cream for my friends.
Luke	Where's Mum? Is she in the garden?
Jessica	No, she isn't. She's in the kitchen. She's making dinner.
25 *Luke*	Great. I'm hungry.
Jessica	You're always hungry, Luke.
Luke	Aren't you hungry?
Jessica	No, I'm not, but I'm thirsty.

1 Luke and Jessica's birthday

1	When is Jessica and Luke's birthday?	<u>next week</u>	next month
2	How old are Jessica and Luke now?	<u>eleven</u>	ten
3	Where is Jessica?	in her room	<u>in Luke's room</u>
4	What is she doing?	<u>She's making a list.</u>	She's writing an e-mail.
5	Where is Jessica and Luke's mum?	in the garden	<u>in the kitchen</u>

2 Before the party

Jessica: 1, 2, 4   Luke: 3, 5, 6

3 Food at the party

1 Luke: pizza, <u>chicken legs</u>, <u>cheese</u>

2 Jessica: <u>chocolate cake</u>, <u>ice cream</u>

> **Lerntipp** So kannst du **Listening Skills** gut üben:
>
> ☐ Höre dir den Text auf der CD noch einmal an.
> ☐ Drücke die Pausentaste jedesmal, wenn Jessica etwas gesagt hat und wiederhole,
>   was sie gesagt hat.

LANGUAGE

1 GRAMMAR The Summers are busy

1 Mum and Dad <u>are working</u> in the kitchen. They <u>aren't working</u> at the restaurant.

2 Mum <u>is making</u> a cake. But she <u>isn't making</u> a chocolate cake.

3 Dad <u>is putting</u> chicken legs on the baking tray. He <u>isn't putting</u> chips on the baking tray.

4 Jessica and Luke <u>are going</u> to the shop together. They <u>aren't arguing</u>.

5 Jessica and Luke <u>are buying</u> some bottles of orange juice. But they <u>aren't buying</u> any milk.

> **Lerntipp** Das **Present-progressive**-Fahrrad
>
> 
>
>
> Fall nicht vom Rad!
> Das **present progressive** hat <u>immer</u>
> ein Vorderrad ▶ **am**, **are**, **is**; **am** / **'m** not; **isn't**; **aren't**
> ein Pedal ▶ **Verb**
> ein Hinterrad ▶ **-ing**.
>
> Wenn du auf das Pedal = **Verb** trittst, dann ist die Handlung im Gang ▶ **present progressive**.
>
> So kannst du üben, das **present progressive** richtig zu bilden:
> Sammle aus deinem Buch oder deinem Workbook Sätze mit dem **present progressive**.
> Zeichne das **Present-progressive**-Fahrrad ein. ▶ Mache einen Kreis (Vorderrad) um **am**, **are**, **is** und einen Kreis (Hinterrad) um **-ing**.
>
> Ergänze das ‚Vorderrad'.

			Zum Überprüfen:
Singular	1. Person	I ◯ not listen**ing** to the radio.	**I am** not listening to the radio.
	2. Person	◯ you listen**ing** to the radio?	**Are** you listening to the radio?
	3. Person	Jessica ◯ tidy**ing** the living room.	Jessica **is** tidying the living room.
		◯ Luke help**ing** her?	**Is** Luke helping her?
Plural	1. Person	We ◯ danc**ing** to the music.	**We are** dancing to the music.
	2. Person	◯ you watch**ing** us?	**Are** you watching us?
	3. Person	They ◯ eat**ing** chips.	**They are** eating chips.

Überprüfe anhand der dritten Spalte, ob du alles richtig hast.

2   WORDS Food for the party

1 *Jessica*   We need <u>some</u> apples and <u>some</u> bananas for a fruit salad.

2 *Luke*   And we haven't got <u>any</u> oranges.

3 *Jessica*   Have we got <u>any</u> biscuits at home?

4 *Luke*   I think we have, but we haven't got <u>any</u> chips.

3   GRAMMAR Are they getting ready for the party?

1 <u>Are Dan and Jo reading their e-mails?</u>

2 <u>Is Jack phoning his friends?</u>

3 <u>Are Sophie and Ananda thinking about presents?</u>

4 <u>Is Ananda making a present?</u>

5 <u>Is Sophie running to a shop?</u>

Lerntipp   Present progressive: questions

So lernst du, **Fragen** im **present progressive** zu bilden:
Sammle Aussagesätze im **present progressive** und bilde daraus Fragesätze.
Sammle Fragesätze (ohne Fragewort) und bilde daraus Aussagesätze.

Present progressive – Aussagesätze Bilde aus diesen Sätzen Fragesätze.		
Singular	1. Person	I **am** sleep**ing** on the floor.
	2. Person	You **are** read**ing** a book.
	3. Person	He **is** sitt**ing** on my bed.
		My hamster **is** drink**ing** water.
		It **is** sitt**ing** in its cage.
Plural	1. Person	We **are** danc**ing** the Hokey Cokey.
	2. Person	You **are** shak**ing** your legs.
	3. Person	They **are** bend**ing** their knees.

Present progressive – Fragesätze
Bilde aus diesen Sätzen Aussagesätze.

Am I sleep**ing** on the floor?
Are you read**ing** a book?
Is he sitt**ing** on my bed?
Is my hamster drink**ing** water?
Is it sitt**ing** in its cage?

Are we danc**ing** the Hokey Cokey?
Are you shak**ing** your legs?
Are they bend**ing** their knees?

4   GRAMMAR Jack's questions

1 <u>What are you doing?</u>

2 <u>What are you talking about?</u>

3 <u>What is Dan doing?</u>

4 <u>Why are Sophie and Ananda reading?</u>

5 <u>Where are they going now?</u>

5 GRAMMAR A present for Jessica and Luke

1 *Sophie*   We need a present for Jessica and Luke. What can we give <u>them</u>?

2 *Ananda*   Jessica likes earrings. We can buy <u>her</u> earrings. But what about Luke?

3 *Jack*   We can buy <u>him</u> an earring too. He can wear <u>it</u> in one ear.

4 *Ananda*   Jack is mad. Don't listen to <u>him</u>, Sophie.

5 *Jack*   Ananda is boring. Don't listen to <u>her</u>, Sophie. Listen to <u>me</u>. My ideas are never boring.

6 *Sophie*   I'm listening to <u>you</u>, Jack. But listen to <u>us</u>: We think an earring for Luke isn't a good idea.

7 *Jack*   OK. What can we buy for <u>him</u>?

6 WORDS In the kitchen

1 You can put milk for the cat in a <u>bowl</u>.

2 Jessica and Luke are buying five <u>bottles</u> of orange juice.

3 There is a <u>jug</u> of water in the fridge.

4 Can I have a <u>glass</u> of water? I'm thirsty.

5 We always put fruit in a <u>basket</u>.

6 There are three <u>packets</u> of crisps on the table.

7 Dad is eating a big <u>piece</u> of pizza. He is very hungry.

8 The cornflakes are in a <u>box</u>.

9 Who is eating cake from my <u>plate</u>?

10 And where is the cheese? It's still in the shopping <u>bag</u>.

WRITING

Hamster Rob is watching the Summer family

I'm sitting here in my cage. I can see Jessica. Jessica isn't cleaning my cage. She is tidying the living room. And Luke? Luke isn't feeding me. He is laying the table. Mrs Summer is in the kitchen. What is she doing? Is she making a cake? Oh! Mr Summer is making a mess. Now Mr and Mrs Summer are arguing. Look! The guests are coming. They are bringing lots of presents for Jessica and Luke. Jessica and Luke are looking at the presents, but they aren't looking at me.

Lerntipp Das **Present-progressive**-Fahrrad	
Lies dir die Musterlösung durch und zeichne das **Present-progressive**-Fahrrad ein. Mache dazu einen Kreis (Vorderrad) um **is / isn't, are / aren't** und einen Kreis (Hinterrad) um **-ing**.	Luke (isn't) feed (ing) me.
Lies dann deine Geschichte und zeichne auch dort das **Present-progressive**-Fahrrad ein. Wo hast du ein Vorderrad oder Hinterrad vergessen? Verbessere diese Sätze.	
Present progressive: Aussagesätze und **Fragesätze** Ordne die **Present-progressive**-Sätze in zwei Spalten:	

Aussagesätze	**Fragesätze**
Luke isn't feeding me. Jessica ...	What is she doing?

3 GRAMMAR The guests are hungry now

1 *Jessica* Would you like <u>some</u> fruit salad, Lisa?

2 *Lisa* Thanks, but I have still got <u>some</u> cake on my plate.

3 *Brian* But I haven't got <u>any</u> cake on my plate. Can I have <u>some</u> fruit salad, please?

4 *Jacob* Can I have <u>some</u> fruit salad too, please?

4 GRAMMAR Hamster Rob and Hamster Ronnie

1 *Rob* <u>What</u> are the kids doing?   *Ronnie* They're dancing the Hokey Cokey.

2 *Rob* But Luke isn't dancing. <u>What</u> is he doing?   *Ronnie* He's eating chicken legs.

3 *Rob* <u>Why</u> is Luke eating chicken legs?   *Ronnie* Because he's hungry.

4 *Rob* <u>Where</u> is Jessica going?   *Ronnie* She's going outside.

5 *Rob* <u>Why</u> is she going outside?   *Ronnie* Because somebody is leaving.

> **Lerntipp** **Present progressive: questions** with **question words**
>
> Unterstreiche in deinen Sätzen das **Fragewort** und zeichne das **Present-progressive**-Fahrrad ein (siehe Lerntipp S. 30). Mache dazu einen Kreis (= Vorderrad) um **is / are** und einen Kreis (= Hinterrad) um **-ing**.

5 GRAMMAR The end of the party

1 *Dan and Jo* It's a great party, Luke. Thanks for inviting <u>us</u>.

2 *Eve* There are so many plates and glasses. I can help <u>you</u>, Jessica.

3 *Jessica* Great! You can help <u>me</u> put <u>them</u> in the dishwasher.

4 *Eve* What about the cake? Where can I put <u>it</u>?

5 *Jessica* Brian loves cake. We can put two pieces in a box for <u>him</u>.

6 *Eve* What about Lisa? Can we give <u>her</u> a piece too?

7 *Jessica* Yes, of course. You can put <u>it</u> in this small box.

8 *Eve* Where are all the kids? Let's find <u>them</u> so they can help <u>us</u>.

> **Lerntipp** **Personal pronouns**
>
> Wie du die **Subjektform** und die **Objektform** der Personalpronomen verwendest, merkst du dir am Besten an einem Beispielsatz: **I love you**. Bilde 5 sinnvolle Sätze.

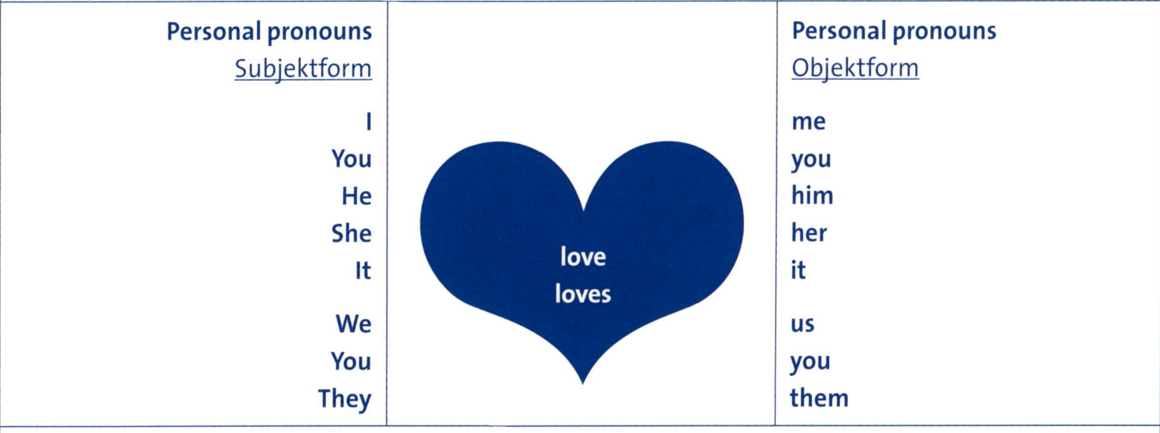

Beispielsätze: **I** love **you / him / her / it / them**. **He / She** loves **me / you / her / him / it / us / them**.

6 WORDS After the party

Luke is <u>in</u> the kitchen, but he doesn't want to help the others. There are lots of plates <u>in</u> the dishwasher. He is going out and he is <u>in</u> a hurry. He is looking <u>at</u> Jessica and Eve but he isn't helping them. Two minutes later he and Jack are getting <u>on</u> the bus. The bus stops <u>at</u> Jack's house and they are getting <u>off</u> the bus. Jack and Luke are having chicken legs <u>with</u> salad <u>for</u> dinner. And what are they talking <u>about</u>? – The second scene of the video project.

GETTING BY IN ENGLISH

Ein Anruf von Andrea Kiefer

Andrea <u>Happy birthday Jessica.</u>

Jessica Thank you, Andrea.

Andrea <u>What are you doing?</u>

Jessica We're dancing.

Andrea <u>Is Luke dancing too?</u>

Jessica No, he isn't. He's in the kitchen with Jack. I think they're talking about our project.

Andrea <u>Why are they talking about a project?</u>

Jessica We're planning a video project: "The Scary Robbers." It's a birthday present from the SHoCK Team.

Andrea <u>That's interesting. What are you doing for the video project?</u>

Jessica I'm a detective. Oh, Jack and Luke are coming back to the living room now.

Andrea <u>Why are they coming back to the living room?</u>

Jessica I think they want to eat the birthday cake.

Andrea <u>But it's your birthday cake too.</u>

Jessica Yes, I know. The boys are eating the cake now. I have to go. I want some cake too!

> **Lerntipp** So kannst du **Getting by in English** üben:
>
> ☐ Unterstreiche in der Lösung Sätze, die dir nicht so gut gelungen sind.
> ☐ Schreibe Ausdrücke, die du dir merken möchtest, in dein Lernheft.

LISTENING

🎧 16 **After the Spring Show**

Sarah	Dad, how did you like our show?
Mr Evans	How did I like the show? What a question, Sarah! The show was fantastic.
Mrs Evans	Yes, it was. I liked the clothes and the music. And I liked Sam, the captain.
Mr Evans	Yes, Sam, you were a great captain and we laughed a lot when you were on stage.
5 *Sam*	You laughed, when I was on stage. But why, Dad? The scene wasn't funny.
Mr Evans	I know it wasn't. But it was so funny when the pirates wanted to catch you. The pirates were so small and you were so – big.
Sam	I know.
Mr Evans	I didn't see you on stage, Sarah.
10 *Sarah*	But I was on stage too, Dad. I was inside the captain's cabin.
Mr Evans	You were inside that big box? Why?
Mrs Evans	Dad, Sarah was the prompter. She had to help the others when they didn't remember their words.
Mr Evans	Did you have to prompt them a lot?
15 *Sarah*	No, Dad, not really. But it was very hot inside the box.
Mr Evans	Were you inside the box too, Sam?
Sam	No, I wasn't. The captain's cabin was too small for two people and a wheelchair. I was next to the box when the pirates came.
Mrs Evans	It was scary when it was dark before the pirates came.
20 *Mr Evans*	Yes, that was great. It was dark and they played scary music and then suddenly the ship was full of pirates.
Mrs Evans	What a great evening it was. And it's so nice to walk home. It isn't windy and it isn't cold. It's a beautiful spring evening. Here we are.
Sam	Are you coming in, Dad?
25 *Mr Evans*	No, sorry, Sam. I have to go back to London.
Sam	Well, thanks for coming, Dad.
Mr Evans	Bye, Sam. Bye, Sarah.
Sam / Sarah	Bye, Dad.

1 The Spring Show

Right: 1, 3, 4, 9   Wrong: 2, 5, 6, 7, 8, 10

2 Why?

1 c; 2 b; 3 c; 4 a; 5 c

> **Lerntipp** So kannst du **Listening Skills** üben:
>
> - Höre dir den Listening-Text noch einmal an.
> - Suche dir eine Rolle aus und sprich diese Rolle mit.

LANGUAGE

1 GRAMMAR After the Spring Show

Our Spring Show <u>was</u> fantastic. We <u>were</u> all very nervous. Jo said he <u>wasn't</u> nervous, but I know he <u>was</u>. And our teacher <u>was</u> nervous too, because there <u>weren't</u> enough costumes, so two pirates <u>were</u> in jeans. They <u>weren't</u> happy about that, but it <u>was</u> OK. After the show everybody <u>was</u> happy and tired.

2 GRAMMAR The Drama Club's report

What a great year for the Drama Club! We <u>had</u> lots of rehearsals for the Spring Show and we <u>made</u> the stage and the pirate ship. Then everything <u>was</u> ready for the big day. We <u>were</u> very nervous. The band <u>played</u> and we all <u>looked</u> great in our costumes. Lots of our parents and teachers <u>came</u> to the show. They <u>said</u> that the Spring Show <u>was</u> fantastic. We <u>were</u> all very happy at the end.

3 GRAMMAR Grandma Scott's questions

1 *Grandma* <u>How was your / the show</u>, Luke? *Luke* It was great.

2 *Grandma* <u>How many people were on stage</u>? *Luke* I think about 40.

3 *Grandma* <u>Were you a pirate</u>? *Luke* Yes, I was.

4 *Grandma* <u>Was Jessica a pirate too</u>? *Luke* No, she was in the choir.

5 *Grandma* <u>Was the choir good</u>? *Luke* No, it wasn't.

4 GRAMMAR Grandpa Scott's questions

1 *Grandpa* <u>Did you like your show?</u> *Jessica* Yes, I did.

2 *Grandpa* <u>Did you sing in the choir?</u> *Jessica* Yes, I did.

3 *Grandpa* <u>Did you sing alone?</u> *Jessica* No, I didn't.

4 *Grandpa* <u>Did you sing songs about pirates?</u> *Jessica* Yes, we did.

5 *Grandpa* <u>Did somebody make a video?</u> *Jessica* Yes, Dad did.

> **Lerntipp** So kannst du üben, Fragen in der Vergangenheit zu bilden.
> Sammle für jeden Beispielkasten zwei Fragen.

Fragen mit **was / were**	Fragen mit **did**
Was ____________________	**Did** ____________________
____________________ ?	____________________ ?
Were ____________________	**Did** ____________________
____________________ ?	____________________ ?

5 GRAMMAR Pretty Polly has got it all wrong

1 *Jack*   That's wrong, Polly. They <u>watched</u> the show.

2 *Jack*   That's wrong, Polly. I <u>played in the band</u>.

3 *Jack*   That's wrong, Polly. The pirates <u>got on the ship</u>.

4 *Jack*   That's wrong, Polly. I <u>saw the pirates</u>.

5 *Jack*   That's wrong, Polly. My friends <u>liked the show</u>.

WRITING

Sophie's diary

Our Spring Show was fantastic, well most of it was fantastic:

In the beginning all the children were nervous. Jack came/was late. Two pirates didn't have costumes.

The choir went to the wrong part of the stage. Mr Kingsley shouted. It was terrible.

The show started ten minutes late, but the stage looked fantastic. First the band played and the choir sang.

Then Sam came on stage. He was the captain.

Suddenly the stage was dark and the pirates climbed on the ship. I was a pirate too. We shouted. The lights

went on again. We pulled the captain out and we all sang our pirate song. It was great.

| **Lerntipp** | So kannst du **Writing Skills** gut üben: |

- Unterstreiche im Lösungstext den ersten Satz in jedem Absatz.
- Unterstreiche in deinem Text den ersten Satz in jedem Absatz.
- Unterstreiche im zweiten Absatz der Musterlösung die Wörter **but**, **first** und **then**.
- Unterstreiche oder ergänze diese Wörter in deinem Text.

READING

International Balloon Festival

1   Find the German meaning

englisches Wort	Hinweis aus dem Bild	deutschem Wort ähnlich	bekanntes Wort enthalten	aus dem Zusammenhang	deutsche Bedeutung
international		✔			international
hot air balloon	✔	✔			Heißluftballon
attraction		✔			Attraction
sensational acrobatics		✔			sensationelle Akrobatik
spectacular finale		✔			spektakuläres Finale
(to) light up			✔	✔	beleuchten

2   Facts about the Bristol International Balloon Festival

1	When is the Balloon Festival?	in spring	in the evening	at a weekend
2	How can you get there?	by car	by train	by balloon
3	How can you get more information?	on the radio	on the internet	by phone

3   Right – Wrong – Not in the text

Right: 7   Wrong: 1, 2, 4, 5   Not in the text: 3, 6

> **Lerntipp**   So kannst du **Reading Skills** üben:
>
> - Erschließe die deutsche Bedeutung der englischen Wörter, die dir unbekannt sind. Dabei hilft dir die Tabelle in Aufgabe 1.
> - Umkreise alle Zahlen und sage, was sie bedeuten.
> - Fasse zusammen, was du über das Balloon Festival weißt.

LANGUAGE

1   GRAMMAR Where were they?

1   Were the Hansons at the swimming pool?   – No, they weren't.

2   Was Jack at the rehearsal?   – Yes, he was.

3   Was Jack's mother in Mr Green's room?   – Yes, she was.

4   Was Mr Hanson in the garden?   – No, he wasn't.

5   Were you at the Spring Show?   – No, I wasn't.

2   GRAMMAR What did they do?

1 Did Dan and Jo go in a balloon?   – No, they didn't.

2 Did Dan and Jo see Ananda?   – Yes, they did.

3 Did Ananda have a picnic with her parents?   – No, she didn't.

4 Did Ananda's parents like the ballons?   – Yes, they did.

5 Did you go to the International Balloon Festival?   – No, I didn't.

> **Lerntipp** Wie du Fragen im **simple past** mit **did** und **Kurzantworten** bildest, kannst du in deinem Schülerbuch (GF 20) nachlesen. Mache auch die Polly-Aufgaben.

3   GRAMMAR Dan's e-mail to Jack

Hi Jack

We <u>had</u> a great time at the International Balloon Festival. We <u>went</u> there by bike. There <u>were</u> lots of balloons in all colours. We <u>talked</u> to the owner of one of the balloons. He <u>told</u> us a lot of interesting things about balloons. We <u>watched</u> how he <u>got</u> his balloon ready. Then there <u>was</u> a big flame and it <u>went</u> up into the sky! It <u>was</u> fantastic!

Dan

> **Lerntipp** Unterstreiche im Lösungstext die regelmäßigen Verben.
> Was du bei regelmäßigen Verben beachten musst, wenn du sie ins **simple past** setzt, kannst du dir im Schülerbuch (GF 18) anschauen. Am besten legst du dir dazu eine Tabelle an.

Regelmäßige Verben im **simple past**:

-ed wird angehängt	stummes e fällt weg	einige Konsonanten werden verdoppelt	y wird zu -ie
look – look**ed** talk – talk**ed** watch – watch**ed** …	use – us**ed** …	stop – stop**ped** …	hurry – hurr**ied** …

4   GRAMMAR International Balloon Festival

1 *Ananda*   Did you go to the International Balloon Festival?

   Dan   Yes, I did. I <u>went</u> there with Jo on Saturday.

2 *Ananda*   I didn't see you there.

   Dan   But we <u>saw</u> you and your parents.

3 *Ananda*   Did you sit on the hill?

   Dan   No, we didn't. We <u>sat</u> on a wall near the balloons.

4 *Ananda*   Did you get information about the balloons?

   Dan   Yes, we did. We <u>got</u> lots of information from the owner of one of the balloons.

5 *Ananda*   What did you do after the Balloon Festival?

   Dan   We phoned Jack and we <u>had</u> a picnic together.

5 PRONUNCIATION Verbs in the simple past

called [kɔːld]	answered, climbed, hoped, played, showed, watched
painted ['peɪntɪd]	added, hated, reported, started

GETTING BY IN ENGLISH

At the International Balloon Festival

Leon	Frag ihn, ob er auch beim Balloon Festival war.
You	Were you at the Balloon Festival too?
David	Yes, my parents and I went there yesterday.
You	Ja, er sagt, dass er gestern mit seinen Eltern dort war.
Leon	Frag ihn, ob es ihm gefallen hat.
You	Did you like it?
David	It was great! Did you see the acrobatics?
You	Er fand es toll. Er fragt, ob wir auch die Akrobatik gesehen haben.
Leon	Sag ihm, dass ich die toll fand.
You	My brother says they were fantastic.
David	Did you go on the go-karts?
Leon	Was fragt er?
You	Er will wissen, ob wir auch Go-Kart gefahren sind.
	We wanted to, but it was too expensive.
Leon	Was erzählst du ihm?
You	Ich habe gesagt, dass wir gerne fahren wollten, es aber zu teuer war.
David	I think the bands were good. Did you like them?
You	Er sagt, dass er die Bands gut fand und fragt, ob wir sie auch mochten.
Leon	Sag ihm, dass die erste schrecklich war, aber die zweite gut war.
You	The first band was terrible, but the second band was good.

LISTENING

🎧 19 Bristol – five attractions

My presentation is about Bristol and about the things you can do in Bristol.

I like Bristol for lots of reasons and I'm going to present five favourite places to you.

Bristol is great for shopping and the first picture shows you the Galleries Shopping Centre. It's a shopping centre with 100 shops in the middle of Bristol. There is Food Street where you can go when you're hungry
5 and choose your favourite food.

When you're tired of shopping you can go to Castle Park. Here in my second picture you can see Bristol 'High Point'. 'High Point' is a helium gas balloon in Castle Park. It can take 30 people about 150 metres up and you can look down and see all of Bristol! It's fantastic.

I like old ships and in my third picture you can see the SS Great Britain. It's about 150 years old. It was the
10 first luxury liner for people with lots of money. Isambard Kingdom Brunel designed this ship.

Isambard Kingdom Brunel designed the Clifton Suspension Bridge too. This is the big bridge in the city of Bristol. You can see this bridge here in my fourth picture. When you're on the bridge, you look down about 70 metres to the river Avon. Yes, it is a little scary.

My last picture shows two kites at Bristol Downs. I really like it here. At the weekends I come here with my
15 friends and we play football. When it's windy, we play with our kites. It's great fun. You can see a lot of Bristol from here, and when it's hot we all buy ice creams from the ice cream man.

There are of course more things you can do and see in Bristol, but my presentation ends here. Thank you for listening.

1 What do the pictures show?

1 D; 2 B; 3 C; 4 E; 5 A

2 Luke's pictures

First picture: C   Second picture: E   Third picture: A   Fourth picture: B   Last picture: D

3 Five different places

1 F, K; 2 A, D, H; 3 B; 4 C, G, L; 5 A, J

Diese beiden Buchstaben gehören nicht dazu: E, I

Lerntipp   So kannst du **Listening Skills** üben:

- Höre dir den Listening-Text noch einmal an.
- Drücke nach jeder Attraktion die Pausentaste und notiere in Stichpunkten, was du dir merken konntest.
- Vergleiche deine Stichpunkte mit dem abgedruckten Listening-Text.
- Unterstreiche im Listening-Text, was du nicht so gut verstanden hast.

LANGUAGE

1   GRAMMAR Shopping

1   Sophie usually <u>goes</u> shopping with her mum, but today she <u>is going</u> shopping with Ananda.

2   Ananda and Sophie are at the Galleries Shopping Centre. They <u>are looking</u> at clothes.

Sophie often <u>buys</u> her clothes at the Galleries, but Ananda <u>doesn't go</u> there very often.

3   Ananda's mother sometimes <u>makes</u> dresses for Ananda, but she <u>doesn't make</u> jeans or T-shirts for her.

4   Ananda <u>isn't wearing</u> a dress today. She is wearing jeans and she <u>is looking for</u> a nice T-shirt or

a sweatshirt.

5   So the two girls <u>are looking</u> at T-shirts and sweatshirts now.

2   WORDS At the Galleries Shopping Centre

a)

1   What about <u>this</u> sweatshirt? <u>It</u>'s nice too.

2   <u>These</u> shoes are great. How much are <u>they</u>?

3   I like the colour of <u>this</u> shirt. <u>It</u>'s my favourite colour.

4   I like <u>these</u> shoes. Are <u>they</u> expensive?

5   <u>This</u> dress is really pretty. How much is <u>it</u>?

b)

1   <u>That</u> top in the magazine is really pretty. Is <u>it</u> expensive?

2   <u>Those</u> socks are funny. I'd like to buy <u>them</u> for Luke.

3   I don't like <u>that</u> shirt – <u>it</u>'s too big.

4   Look at <u>those</u> boots. <u>They</u>'re really great.

5   I don't like <u>that</u> dress because <u>it</u>'s purple.

3   GRAMMAR The International Balloon Festival at Bristol

1   Last week there <u>was</u> the International Balloon Festival at Ashton Court Bristol.

2   Lots of people <u>were</u> there and the Summer Family <u>went</u> there too.

3   Luke and Jessica <u>saw</u> lots and lots of balloons.

4   Mr Summer <u>took</u> photos and the kids <u>had</u> ice cream.

5   Mrs Summer <u>didn't have</u> ice cream.

6   She <u>went</u> to a nice place under a tree.

7   She <u>sat</u> down and <u>made</u> some sandwiches.

GETTING BY IN ENGLISH

At the Galleries Shopping Centre

Du willst wissen,

… wie oft sie hier einkaufen gehen?

How often do you go shopping here?

… was sie hier normalerweise kaufen?

What do you usually buy here?

… ob Kleidung hier sehr teuer ist?

Are clothes very expensive here?

… ob sie dir ein Geschäft zeigen können, wo man Souvenirs (= souvenirs) kaufen kann?

Can you show me a shop where you can buy souvenirs?

… wann ihre Sommerferien anfangen?

When do your summer holidays start?

… ob sie an der Schule Deutsch lernen?

Do you learn German at school?

… ob du ein Foto von ihnen machen darfst?

Can I take a photo of you?

Du willst sagen, dass …

… du ihnen die Fotos schicken kannst.

I can send you the photos.

… du Bristol aus vielen Gründen magst.

I like Bristol for lots of reasons.

… du in einem kleinen Dorf in Deutschland wohnst.

I live in a small village in Germany.

> **Lerntipp** So kannst du **Getting by in English** gut üben:
>
> - Schreibe die Sätze, die dir nicht so gut gelungen sind, in dein Lernheft.
> - Übe die Sätze, bei denen du Schwierigkeiten hattest, einen Tag später noch einmal.
> - Überlege dir, was du Sophie und Ananda noch fragen könntest, und schreibe diese Fragen auf Englisch auf.

READING

An e-mail from Germany

1   The farm

Right: 2, 3   Wrong: 1, 5   Not in the text: 4

2   The children

Andrea: 2   Jessica: 3, 6   Luke: 5   Susanne: 1, 3, 4

3   What did the children do together …?

1   They explored the tower / the place.

2   They played with the boats.

3   They had chocolate cake.

> **Lerntipp**   So kannst du **Reading Skills** üben:
>
> ☐ Umkreise alle Namen im Text. Nimm für jeden Namen eine andere Farbe.
> ☐ Ordne den Personen zu, was sie machen. Die Aktivität unterstreichst du in derselben Farbe.

LANGUAGE

1   WORDS Old toys

1   *Andrea*   Look at these little teddy bears. Aren't they nice?

2   *Jessica*   I like this bear, but I don't like that bear. It hasn't got any legs.

3   *Luke*   I like these boats. Those old bears are for girls.

4   *Susanne*   All these toys must be very old. We can take this bear and that little boat.

5   *Luke*   Why don't we take these four boats and put those bears back in the box?

2   GRAMMAR Under the bridge

1   It was windy when the kids took the boats to the river.

2   But the kids enjoyed it because each boat sailed in the wind.

3   Only Andrea was sad when she saw that there was a hole in her boat.

4   Luke's boat was very good because it had a big sail.

5   They went back to the farm house because they were hungry.

> **Lerntipp**   So kannst du üben, **Nebensätze** mit **when** und **because** richtig zu bilden:
>
> ☐ Lies die Grammar File 21 in deinem Schulbuch.
> ☐ Mache die Polly-Aufgabe der Grammar File 21.
> ☐ Übersetze die Polly-Sätze der Grammar File 21 und vergleiche die Satzstellung im Englischen mit der Satzstellung im Deutschen.

3   GRAMMAR The Kiefer family

a)

1   It's 7.30 pm. Mr Kiefer <u>is sitting</u> in front of the TV.

2   Tonight he <u>is watching</u> a football match. Eintracht Frankfurt <u>are playing</u> Dynamo Dresden.

3   Mrs Kiefer and Andrea <u>aren't watching</u> TV. They <u>are making</u> a chocolate cake.

b)

1   Mrs Kiefer <u>doesn't like</u> football. In the evening she often <u>goes</u> jogging with a friend.

2   Andrea and Mr Kiefer sometimes <u>watch</u> a football match together.

3   Mr Kiefer <u>watches</u> lots of football matches and he <u>plays</u> football in a club.

Lerntipp	Simple present oder present progressive?

- Lies Grammar File 22 in deinem Schulbuch.
- Mache die Polly-Aufgabe der Grammar File 22.

WRITING

Mrs Summer's e-mail

Hi Jessica, hi Luke,

I'm worried. How is your leg, Luke? Is it really OK again? Can you walk? Does it hurt? What happened?

Why did you climb on the bridge?

In your e-mail you told me about this girl Susanne. How old is she? Is she in Andrea's form?

You went to her farm. Do they have animals on the farm? Do her parents both work on the farm?

You played under a bridge. How big is this bridge and how big is this river? And then this tower!

Why is there a tower on the farm? How old is this tower? Does it have windows and doors?

Who put this old box in the tower?

Please write soon.

Here everything is OK.

Love, Mum

Lerntipp	So kannst du Writing Skills üben:

- Unterstreiche in den Lösungen die Aussagesätze.
- Zähle, wie viele Fragen inhaltlich zu jedem Aussagesatz gehören.
- Überprüfe in deinem Text, wo du Aussagesätze und wo du Fragesätze geschrieben hast.

Klassenarbeit A

Unit 2

Gesamtpunktzahl _______ / 70   Note _______

READING

_______ / 20

A day in the life of Luke Summer

by Luke Summer

My family has got a restaurant: *The Summer Place.*
Dad gets up early every morning because he gets
things ready for the restaurant. A restaurant is
a lot of work. It opens at 10.30. Mum makes
5 breakfast. She gets up early too. Jessica is my
twin sister. She gets up after Mum and I get up
after my sister. She has a shower every morning
and she is in the bathroom for half an hour. Girls!
After breakfast we go to school. We come home
10 at 4 o'clock. Then Jessica does her homework,
but I first watch TV and then I do my homework.
Mum and Dad aren't at home in the afternoon.
They work at the restaurant.

I like our restaurant and at the weekends I
15 sometimes help Dad in the kitchen. The guests
like Dad's food and he likes his guests. In the
evening Mum comes home at 7.30. She brings
food from the restaurant and we eat together.
Dad doesn't eat with us. He eats at the restaurant.
20 I go to bed after Jessica. She goes to bed at 8.30,
but I go to bed at 9.00. Sometimes I listen to
music before I go to bed. Dad comes home very
late at night.

1   Luke's parents

_______ / 8

Right – Wrong – Not in the text. Tick the correct box.

		Right	Wrong	Not in the text
1	The Summers live over a restaurant.	☐	☐	☐
2	Luke's mum and dad get up early.	☐	☐	☐
3	Luke's dad makes breakfast.	☐	☐	☐
4	He has got a lot to do for the restaurant.	☐	☐	☐
5	He comes home late at night.	☐	☐	☐
6	Luke's mother works at the restaurant too.	☐	☐	☐
7	She helps in the kitchen.	☐	☐	☐
8	She eats at the restaurant.	☐	☐	☐

2   Luke or Jessica?

_______/8

Draw lines from the sentences to Luke or Jessica.

1   doesn't get up early

2   takes a long time in the bathroom

3   has breakfast

4   goes to school

5   comes home at 4 o'clock

6   watches TV first

7   helps in the restaurant

8   goes to bed early

3   The restaurant

_______/4

Complete the sentences.

1   The name of the restaurant is ____.

2   The restaurant opens at ____________________________.

3   _Luke_   The guests like ____________________.   Dad likes ____________________.

LANGUAGE

_______/ 30

1   GRAMMAR Luke's friends at school

_______/5

Fill in. Ergänze die richtigen Possessivbegleiter.

> my (2x) • your • his (2x) • her • its • our • their (2x)

1   I'm in Form 7JM, but ____________ new friends are in Form 7PK.

2   This is Dan and ____________ twin brother Jo.

3   They are nice, and ____________ jokes are great.

4   Jack is ____________ friend too.

5   ____________ dad has got a Bed and Breakfast and a parrot.

6   ____________ cage is in the kitchen.

7   This is Ananda and ____________ friend Sophie.

8   ____________ friends are Dan, Jo and Jack too.

9   ____________ school is a big school.

10   What about you? Is ____________ school big too?

2   GRAMMAR / WORDS Who is who in Luke's family?   _____ / 5

Complete the sentences.

Beispiel: Jessica is Luke's <u>sister</u>.

1   Luke is Jessica's _________________________.

2   Andrea is Jessica and Luke's _________________________.

3   Jessica is Mary and Joe's _________________________.

4   Jane Kiefer and Bob Scott are Luke's _________________________.

5   Bob Scott is Grandma and Grandpa Scott's _________________________.

3   WORDS Luke and his family   _____ / 5

Look at Luke's family and find the right words.

1   Mary and Joe are my p_________________. They are married. They are not d_________________.

2   Emma, Jacob, Jessica and I are Grandma and Grandpa Scott's g_________________.

3   Grandma Summer and Grandpa Summer are d_________________.

4   Emma, Jacob and Andrea are my c_________________.

4 GRAMMAR It's the same[1] every day!

_____/5

Complete Jessica's sentences. Fill in the right verb in the right form.

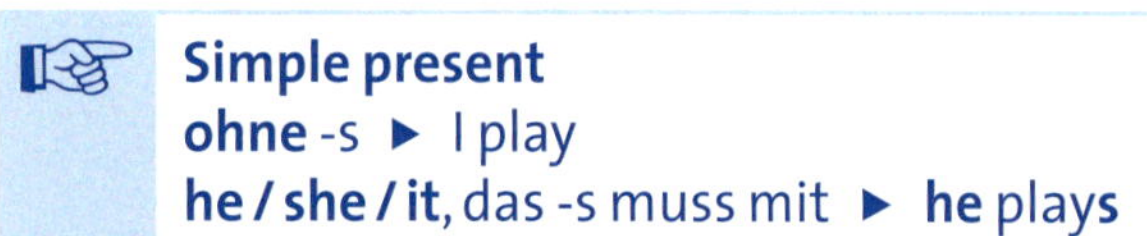

1 I ______________ a shower every morning, Luke ______________ a shower every evening.

2 I ______________ my homework in the afternoon, Luke ______________ his homework in the evening.

3 I ______________ my room every day, and Luke ______________ his room every week.

4 I ______________ to the rabbit hutch, Luke ______________ to his friends.

5 I ______________ with my rabbits, Luke ______________ football with his friends.

> 👉 **Simple present**
> **ohne** -s ▶ I play
> **he / she / it**, das -s muss mit ▶ **he** plays

5 GRAMMAR The Summer family

_____/5

Write what they do and what they don't do.

1 Luke ______________________ (not / do) judo. He ______________ (play) football.

2 Jessica ______________________ (not / play) football. She ______________ (have) music lessons.

3 Mr and Mrs Summer ______________________ (not / have) time at weekends.

   They ______________ (work) at the restaurant.

4 *Aunt Jane* I ______________________ (not / live) in England.

   My family and I ______________ (live) in Germany.

5 Andrea ______________ (speak) English with her mum, but she ______________________ (not / speak)

   English with her dad.

> 👉 **Simple present – Verneinung**
> 1. Person Singular   I ▶ **don't** live
> 3. Person Singular   he / she ▶ **doesn't** do
> 3. Person Plural   they ▶ **don't** have

 the same [seɪm] *das Gleiche*

6   WORDS   The Summers and their friends

_____/5

Find the missing adjectives.

1   Mr Summer's friend isn't married and he doesn't have a girlfriend. He is s_____________.

2   Sam is Luke's friend. His parents aren't together. They are d_____________.

3   Luke thinks History is boring. But Jessica thinks it is i_____________________.

4   Mrs Summer's friend doesn't like cold tea. She only likes her tea h_____________.

5   German is easy for Mr Kiefer, but he thinks English is d_________________________.

WRITING

_____/ 20

 **A morning in my family**

What do you do every morning? What don't you do?
What about your mum, your dad, brothers, sisters or grandparents?
Complete the mind map with three of them and write eight sentences.
The ideas in the box can help you.

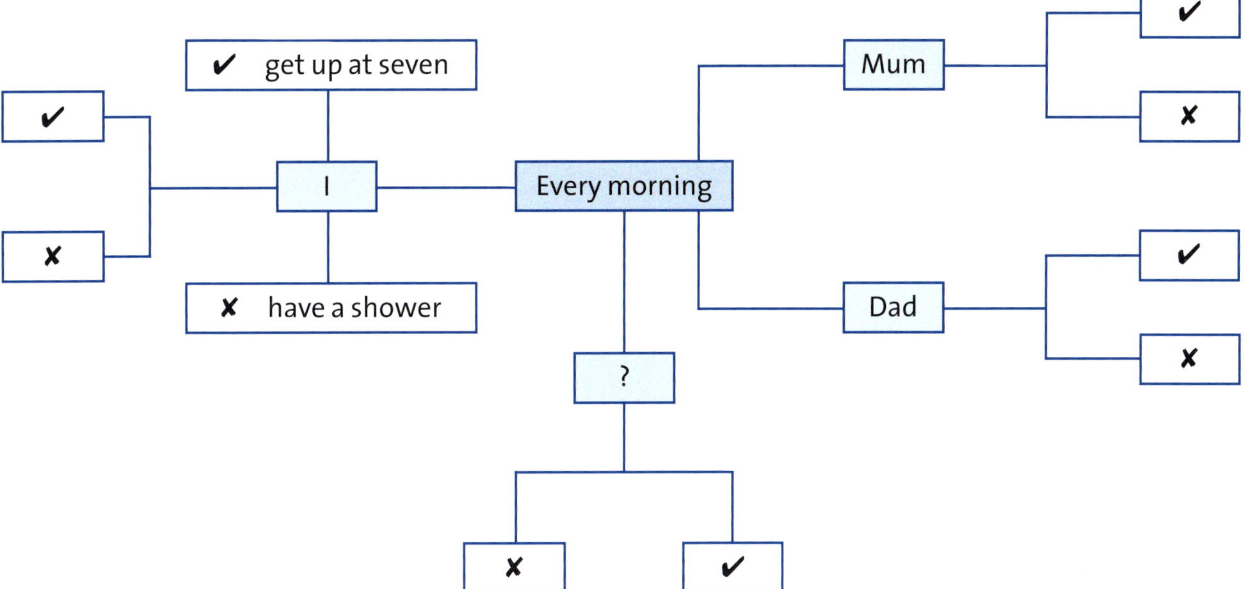

Ideas:
get up • clean my teeth • have a shower • get dressed • make my bed • get things ready • make breakfast • have breakfast • read newspaper • feed pets • go to school • go to work

Du kannst deine Sätze mit **I, Mum, Mum and Dad** beginnen.
Du kannst Sätze auch mit **Then I, Sometimes I, After that I** beginnen.

Klassenarbeit B

Gesamtpunktzahl _______ / 65   Note _______

LISTENING

_____/ 15

🎧 07 **In the Scotts' garden**

Andrea Kiefer and Jacob Scott are in the Scotts' garden. Listen to Andrea and Jacob.

👉 Du kannst diese Aufgabe auch als **Reading**-Aufgabe machen.
Den Text findest du auf Seite 17 im **Lösungsheft** abgedruckt.

1   What pets have they got?

_____/4

Make four ticks (✔) in the correct boxes.

	cat	dog	guinea pigs	hamsters	rabbits
Andrea					
The Scotts					

2   Who feeds these pets?

_____/4

Make four ticks (✔) in the correct boxes.

	cat	dog	guinea pigs	hamsters	rabbits
Andrea					
Jacob					
Emma					
Mrs Scott					
Mr Scott					

3 Right or wrong?

_______/7

Tick the correct box.

		Right	Wrong
1	The hamsters' names are *Blacky* and *Browny*.	☐	☐
2	Mr Scott cleans the hutch every Saturday.	☐	☐
3	*Stella* is the dog's name.	☐	☐
4	The dog is four years old.	☐	☐
5	The dog eats Jacob's books.	☐	☐
6	Andrea and Jacob run up and down the stairs.	☐	☐
7	Andrea hasn't got a brother or a sister.	☐	☐

LANGUAGE

_______/ 30

1 GRAMMAR The Scott family

_______/ 5

*Use the verb in the **simple present** and complete the sentences.*

1   In the morning Mr Scott ______________ (get up) early and ______________ (read) the newspaper.

2   Mrs Scott ______________________ (not / read) the newspaper. She ______________ (make) breakfast.

3   Jacob and Emma ______________ (get up) after their parents. They ______________________

(not / make) breakfast.

4   After breakfast Mr Scott ______________ (tidy) the kitchen before he ______________ (go) to work.

5   Mrs Scott ______________________ (not / tidy) the kitchen. She ____________ (take)

Emma to kindergarden.

2   GRAMMAR A letter from Andrea

______/5

Find the possessive determiners! Verwende nur die Possessivbegleiter!

> my • your • you're • his • he's • her • its • it's • our • their • they're

Hi Jacob,

1   How is ____________ new school? ____________ school is OK.

2   We've got two new guinea pigs. ____________ cage is in ____________ living room.

3   And I've got a rabbit. ____________ rabbit's name is *Pearl*. ____________ hutch is in the garden.

4   Mum likes ____________ garden, Dad likes ____________ car and I like ____________ pets.

5   What about ____________ pets?

Love, Andrea

3   GRAMMAR Mrs Kiefer and Mrs Scott

______/5

Complete the sentences.

1   *Mrs Kiefer*   I ____________ (get up) at 6 o'clock every morning.

   Mrs Scott   I ________________ (not / get up) so early.

2   *Mrs Kiefer*   Herbert ____________ (have) coffee for breakfast, but I ____________ (have) tea.

   Mrs Scott   Bob ________________ (not / like) coffee, but I ____________ (like) it.

3   *Mrs Kiefer*   Herbert ____________ (take) Andrea to school. School ____________ (start) at 8 o'clock.

   Mrs Scott   Bob ________________ (not / take) Jacob to school.

   School ________________ (not / start) at 8 o'clock.

4   GRAMMAR Jacob and Andrea

______/5

How do you write the s-sound? 's or s'

1   *Andrea*   Where are your rabbits? Are they in a hutch?

   Jacob   Yes, the rabbit___ hutch is in the garden, but the dog___ basket is in the house.

2   *Andrea*   Is this Emma___ room?

   Jacob   No, it isn't. It's Mum and Dad___ room.

3   *Andrea*   Your desk is very old.

   Jacob   It is Grandpa Scott___ desk.

5 WORDS Food for the cat

_____ / 5

Complete the dialogue. Use:

> bowl • hear • here you are • meat • of course •
> please • remember • sorry • thanks • think

1 *Mr Scott*   Jacob, you can feed the cat and I can read my book.

   Can you give me my glasses, ______________________.

   Jacob   Yes, ________________, Dad. __________________

2 *Mr Scott*   __________________, Jacob.

   Jacob   Where is the cat food?

3 *Mr Scott*   __________________, I can't __________________ you.

   Jacob   The cat food. Where is it?

4 *Mr Scott*   Oh! I don't __________________. I __________________ it's in the cupboard.

   Jacob   There's a tin[1] of __________________.

5 *Mr Scott*   That's right. Open it and put it in a __________________.

6 WORDS An afternoon in the garden

_____ / 5

Find the plural forms.

1 The Scott <u>family</u> and the Kiefer <u>family</u> are together. The two __________________ are in the garden.

2 Andrea can see a <u>mouse</u> under the tree. There are lots of __________________ in the garden.

3 There are __________________ in the pond[2]. One <u>fish</u> is really big.

4 The __________________ are hungry and one <u>child</u> is very hungry.

5 That's Emma. She has got a pizza <u>box</u>. There are more pizza __________________ in the kitchen.

[1] tin *Dose*   [2] pond *Teich*

GETTING BY IN ENGLISH

_____ / 20

Sundays

Andrea Kiefer spricht gut Englisch, weil ihre Mutter Engländerin ist. Sie spricht auch gut Deutsch, weil sie in Deutschland aufwächst. Mit ihren Eltern ist sie zu Besuch bei englischen Verwandten und muss für ihren Vater dolmetschen.

Bob Scott   I like Sundays. On Sundays I don't get up early, I don't go to work, I don't sit at my desk.

On Sundays there is enough time to be with the family.

Herbert Kiefer   Was sagt er da? Heute ist doch gar nicht Sonntag.

Andrea   Onkel Bob hat gesagt, ____

____

____

____

Herbert Kiefer   Der hat's gut! Sag ihm mal, dass das bei uns anders ist: Papa steht früh auf und sitzt am

Schreibtisch. Er arbeitet auch am Sonntag und er macht das Frühstück.

Andrea   Well, Sundays are different for Dad. He ________________________________

____

____

Bob Scott   Well, after breakfast I work in my garden. Sometimes the kids help me in the garden.

Jacob feeds the rabbits or climbs the trees and Emma plays in her little garden house.

Herbert Kiefer   Er arbeitet im Garten?

Andrea   Ja, nach dem Frühstück arbeitet er im Garten. ________________________

____

____

____

Bob Scott   Sunday afternoons we go to Grandma and Grandpa's house.

Andrea   Sonntagnachmittag ____

Herbert Kiefer   Und was machen sie am Abend?

Andrea   ____

Bob Scott   We sometimes play board games (= Brettspiele) or watch TV together.

Andrea   ____

____

Klassenarbeit A

Unit 3

Gesamtpunktzahl ______ / 65   Note ______

LISTENING

_____ / 15

🎧 10 **Sport and hobbies**

Andrea from Germany visits her cousin Luke in England. Listen to Luke and Andrea.

☞   Du kannst diese Aufgabe auch als **Reading**-Aufgabe machen.
Lies dazu den Text im **Lösungsheft**, S. 22, und bearbeite dann die Aufgaben.

1   What do they do in their free time?

_____ / 5

Put five ticks (✔) in the correct boxes.

	plays football	plays the guitar	plays hockey	rides horses	watches sport on TV	is in a club
Andrea's dad						
Andrea						
Luke						

2   Andrea and her friends

_____ / 7

*Tick **right** or **wrong**.*

		Right	Wrong
1	Sascha and Monika are Andrea's neighbours.		
2	Their parents have got a farm[1].		
3	Sascha thinks horses are scary.		
4	The horses run away from him.		
5	Andrea hasn't got a horse.		
6	Pax and Laurette are old horses.		
7	Andrea often rides Ambassador.		

[1] farm [fɑːm] *Bauernhof*

3 What does Andrea do on the farm?

_____ / 3

Tick three pictures.

LANGUAGE

_____ / 30

1 GRAMMAR At a sports club

_____ /7

What do they do (✔)? What don't they do (✘)? Complete the sentences.

	play	play	do	go swimming
Julian	✔		✘	
Esther		✘		✔
Sven + Britta		✔		✘
The Devlins	✘		✔	
Naomi	✔	✘		
The Browns		✔	✘	

1 Julian ______________ ______________, but he ______________________________.

2 Esther ______________________, but she ______________________.

3 Sven and Britta ______________________, but they ______________________.

4 The Devlins ______________________, but they ______________________.

5 Naomi ______________________, but she ______________________.

6 The Browns ______________________, but they ______________________.

7 And you? I ______________________, but I ______________________.

☞ **Simple present** ▸ **Aussagesätze**

2. Person Singular	you	▸ play	▸ don't play
3. Person Singular	he / she	▸ play**s**	▸ **doesn't** play
3. Person Plural	they	▸ play	▸ don't play

2 GRAMMAR What sport do they do?

_____/4

Make questions and complete the short answers.

Example: Mark goes swimming. (his brother / go swimming / too)?

Does his brother go swimming too?   Yes, he _does._

1   The Millers play hockey. (the Coopers / play hockey / too)?

____. No, they ____________.

2   Anna and Sabrina go riding. (Claudia / go riding / too)?

____. No, she ____________.

3   Toby plays table tennis. (his parents / play table tennis / too)?

____. No, they ____________.

4   We do sport at school. (you / do sport at school / too)?

____. Yes, I ____________.

☞ **Simple present** ▸ **Fragesätze** mit **do / does**

2. Person Singular	**Do** you do …?
3. Person Singular	**Does** he go …? ▸ kein **s** am <u>Verb</u>!
3. Person Plural	**Do** they play …?

Kurzantworten
Yes, I **do**. / No, I **don't**.
Yes, he **does**. / No, he **doesn't**.
Yes, they **do**. / No, they **don't**.

---

3 GRAMMAR How often do you go swimming?

_____/4

Look at the answers and write the questions.

Example: (How often / Mark / go swimming)?   – Every Tuesday.

How often does Mark go swimming?

1   (When / the Millers / play hockey)?   – At the weekend.

____.

2   (Where / Anna and Sabrina / go riding)?   – On a farm.

____.

3   (Why / Toby / play table tennis)?   – Because he likes table tennis.

____.

4   (How often / Lisa and Toby / play table tennis)?   – Every Friday.

____.

☞ **Simple present** ▸ **Fragesätze** mit **Fragewort**

| 3. Person Singular | **Fragewort + does** he <u>play</u> …? ▸ kein **s** am <u>Verb</u>! |
| 3. Person Plural | **Fragewort + do** they play…? |

4 GRAMMAR Who has to feed the horses?

_____ / 5

*Use **have to / has to** or **don't have to / doesn't have to** and complete the sentences.*

1 *Anna* I ________________________________ (feed) the horses, but I

________________________________ (not / clean) their boxes.

2 *Sabrina* No, Anna. You ________________________________ (clean) the boxes but you

________________________________ (not / feed) the horses.

3 *Mr Rider* We all ________________________________ (clean) the boxes and we all

________________________________ (feed) the horses.

4 *Mr Rider* Ted ________________________________ (take) the horses back to the box, the girls

________________________________ (not / do) that.

5 *Mr Rider* They ________________________________ (make) sandwiches, Ted can help them,

but he ________________________________ (not / help).

5 GRAMMAR Prunella and Uncle Henry

_____ / 5

Make a ✔ where you can put the adverb.

	Adverbs
1 Prunella plays tennis with uncle Henry.	(sometimes)
2 They play with rackets.	(usually)
3 Uncle Henry doesn't have a head, so Prunella wins.	(always)
4 The neighbours call the police.	(never)
5 But they shout at them because of the noise.	(often)

6 STUDY SKILLS Make a dictionary

_____ / 5

Put the words in the right position.

skate • sink • share • sell • single • shoe • sing • shirt • shop • size

se – sh	
si – sk	

GETTING BY IN ENGLISH

_____ / 20

My free time activities

Jack ist Adrians neuer Brieffreund. Er will ihm schreiben, was er in seiner Freizeit macht.
Adrian stellt Jack auch einige Fragen, um herauszufinden, was Jack in seiner Freizeit macht.
Schreibe Adrians Brief. Die Notizen helfen dir.

Adrians Freizeit
Computerspiele / immer abends / nach Hausaufgaben
Mama mag das nicht / Papa spielt manchmal mit.

____

____

____

Adrians Lieblingssport
Fußball / Mittwoch und Samstag / normalerweise Spiele am Samstag / gutes Team /
viel Spaß / gewinnen nicht immer / Papa mag Fußball, aber spielt nicht / Fußballspiele
im Fernsehen

____

____

____

Adrians Fragen an Jack
Adrian will wissen, was Jack in seiner Freizeit macht, was er nach der Schule macht und
was sein Lieblingssport ist.

____

____

☞ Verwende in deinem Brief auch Häufigkeitsadverbien:
always, never, sometimes, usually, often

Hi Jack,
In my free time ...
Love, ...

Gesamtpunktzahl _______ / 70   Note _______

READING

_______ / 20

What I do in my free time

by Sarah Evans

Most people think I can't do a sport because I'm in a
wheelchair and because I can't walk or run. But I like
sport and I play basketball in a team. People usually can't
understand how you can play basketball when you are in
5 a wheelchair, but I'm really good at it, you know. In our
group we are all in wheelchairs. We push our wheelchairs,
we turn our wheelchairs, we shout, we try to catch[1] the
ball, we throw the ball to a partner or into the basket. It is
a lot of noise and a lot of fun. People think it is scary when
10 they first watch us and see how quick we are. But it isn't
scary for us. We are a mad group. Nine girls and Bob.
He's the only boy. He's really funny.

We meet every Tuesday and Friday evening at a place
called Anyway. I can't go there by bus, so Mum has to take
15 me in the car. It isn't easy for her because she works in a
shop and she usually works till eight in the evening. But
on Tuesdays and Fridays she comes home at five. We have
tea and a sandwich. We leave the house at 5.30 and our
training starts at 6 pm.

20 Yes, there are lots of things I can't do. At school I can't do
sport. I can only sit and watch and I have to stay at home
when the other kids go skating in the afternoon. But at
least I can play basketball and that's great. It is very
important to me.

1 Sarah

_______ / 10

Tick (✔) the correct box.

		Right	Wrong	Not in the text
1	Sarah is in a wheelchair.			
2	Bob is in a wheelchair too.			
3	He is at Sarah's school.			
4	Sarah likes sport.			
5	Sarah is very good at basketball.			
6	She plays basketball at school.			
7	Training starts at 5.30.			
8	Sarah never eats before her training.			
9	Her trainer is clever.			
10	Her team often wins matches.			

[1] (to) catch [kætʃ] _fangen_

2　Sarah's mum

_______ / 5

Find the missing information.

1　Sarah's mum works in ____.

2　She usually works till _____________________ o'clock in the evening.

3　But on _____________________ and Fridays she is home at _____________________ o'clock.

4　She eats a _____________________ before they go to Sarah's training.

3　Sarah and basketball

_______ / 5

Tick the right answer or answers.

	Right	Wrong
1　Why do most people think Sarah can't play basketball?		
a)　She is too young.	☐	☐
b)　She can't run.	☐	☐
c)　She is a scary girl.	☐	☐

	Right	Wrong
2　What does Sarah do when she plays basketball?		
a)　She pushes and turns her wheelchair.	☐	☐
b)　She talks with Bob.	☐	☐
c)　She shouts a lot.	☐	☐

	Right	Wrong
3　What do people think when they first watch Sarah's team play basketball?		
a)　It is boring.	☐	☐
b)　They can't play.	☐	☐
c)　It's scary.	☐	☐

	Right	Wrong
4　What does Sarah think about basketball?		
a)　It's too much hard work.	☐	☐
b)　It makes me happy.	☐	☐
c)　It's a team sport.	☐	☐

LANGUAGE

_____ / 30

1 GRAMMAR At the shop

_____ / 5

Read Mrs Turner's answers. Then write Mr Cox' questions.

1 **Mr Cox**   (where – you – put – T-shirts)? _______________________________________

   Mrs Turner   I put them on the shelves.

2 **Mr Cox**   (when – Miss Broom – clean – shelves)?

   ____

   Mrs Turner   Miss Broom cleans the shelves every Monday.

3 **Mr Cox**   (what – Mr Cheap – do)?   _______________________________________

   Mrs Turner   Mr Cheap gets everything ready for the next week.

4 **Mr Cox**   (How often – you – sell – dresses)?

   ____

   Mrs Turner   We don't sell dresses very often.

5 **Mr Cox**   (Why – we – have – a lot of dresses – then)?

   ____

   Mrs Turner   I don't know.

> ☞ **Simple present ▸ Fragesätze mit Fragwort**
>
> 2. Person Singular   **Fragewort + do** you sell ...?
> 3. Person Singular   **Fragewort + does** he do? ▸ kein **s** am Verb!
> 1. Person Plural   **Fragewort + do** we have ...?

2 GRAMMAR The Turners at home

_____ / 5

What do they have to do? Make sentences. Use **have to** or **has to**.

> Mum + Dad: go to work • Tina: go to school / clean the cage • Dad: go shopping
> Tina + Dad: feed the hamsters • Mum: make dinner

1 ____.

2 ____.

3 ____.

4 ____.

5 ____.

> ☞ **müssen: has to – have to**
>
> 3. Person Singular   he / she ▸ **has to** go
> 3. Person Plural   they ▸ **have to** go

3 GRAMMAR What don't they have to do?

_____/5

Look at the list in exercise 2. What don't they have to do?

1 Tina doesn't have to go to work and she ____.

2 Mum and Dad don't have to go to school and they ________________________________.

3 Mum ____.

4 Dad ____.

5 Tina and Dad ____.

> ☞ **nicht** <u>müssen</u>: **doesn't** <u>have to</u> – **don't** <u>have to</u>
>
> 3. Person Singular   he / she ▶ **doesn't** <u>have to</u> go
> 3. Person Plural   they ▶ **don't** <u>have to</u> go

4 GRAMMAR The Carter-Browns – what do they have to do?

_____/ 10

Write questions and complete the short answers.

Example: Toby has to help his dad in the garden. (Sophie / help / garden)?

Does Sophie have to help her dad in the garden?   No, she _doesn't._

1 Sophie has to feed the pets. (Toby / feed / pets)?

____. Yes, he ____________.

2 Emily and Toby have to clean the bathroom. (Dad and Sophie)?

____. No, they ____________.

3 Dad has to wash the car. (Mum / wash / car)?

____. No, she ____________.

4 Mum and Dad have to go to work. (Emily / Sophie / Toby)?

____. No, they ____________.

5 _Sophie_   I have to help my mum in the kitchen. (You / help / your mum / kitchen)?

____. Yes, I ____________.

> ☞ **Simple present ▶ Fragesätze** mit **do / does + have to**
>
> 2. Person Singular   **Do**   you   **have to** …?
> 3. Person Singular   **Does** he / she **have to** …? ▶ kein s am Verb!
> 3. Person Plural   **Do**   they   **have to** …?
>
> **Simple present ▶ Kurzantworten**
>
> 2. Person Singular   Yes, I **do.**   No, I **don't.**
> 3. Person Singular   Yes, he **does.** No she **doesn't.**
> 3. Person Plural   No, they **don't.**

5 GRAMMAR Poor Sophie

_______ / 5

Make sentences. Put the words in the right place.

1   I – have to – help – Mum – in the kitchen – always

____

2   Toby – has to – help – Mum – in the kitchen – never

____

3   He – can – play – in his room – in the garden – often – or

____

4   Emily – goes – shopping – Mum – sometimes – with

____

5   Emily – comes – home – new clothes – usually – with

____

WRITING

_______ / 20

 **The Life of Brian Moody**

Look at the mind map, complete it and then write about Brian. What does he have to do at home or at school?
What can he do at home or at school? What does he often, sometimes or never do with his friends?
You can also write what Brian doesn't have to do, what he can't do and what he doesn't do.

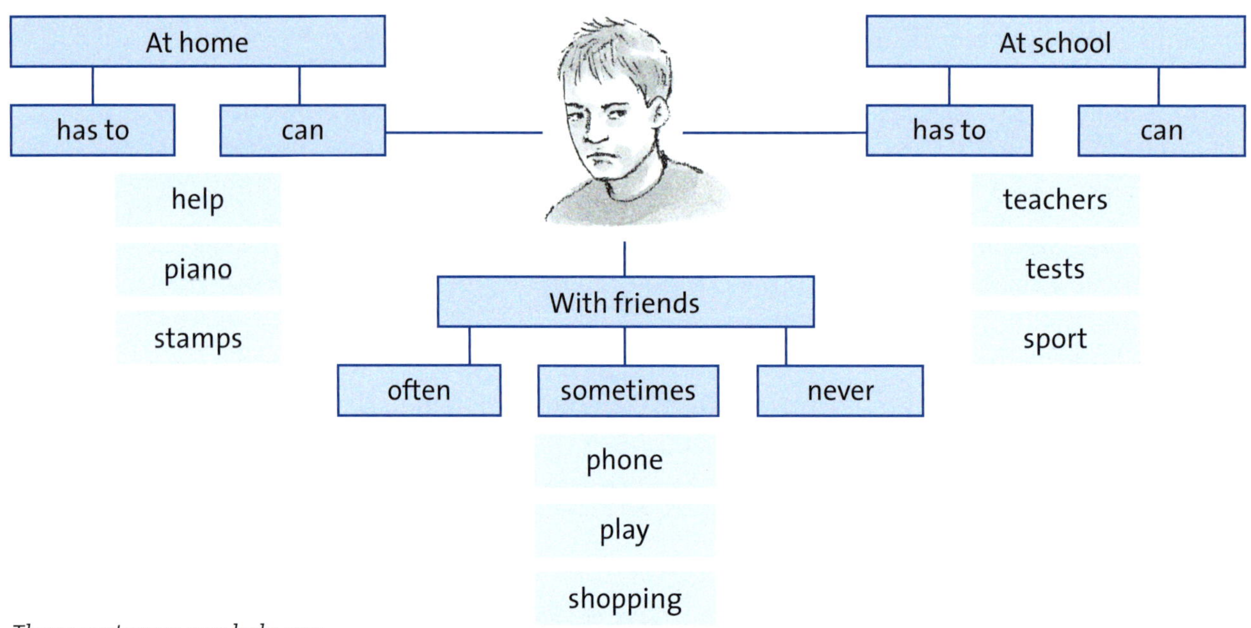

These sentences can help you:

This is Brian's life:
– At home he <u>has to</u> help his mum.
– At school he <u>can</u> do sport.
– He never <u>goes</u> shopping with friends.

Klassenarbeit A — Unit 4

Gesamtpunktzahl _______ / 65   Note _______

LISTENING

_______ / 15

🎧 13 An invitation list

Listen to Jessica and Luke.

☞ Du kannst diese Aufgabe auch als **Reading**-Aufgabe machen. Den Text findest du auf Seite 29 im **Lösungsheft** abgedruckt.

1 Luke and Jessica's birthday

_______ / 5

Underline the right answer.

		Answer 1	Answer 2
1	When is Jessica and Luke's birthday?	next week	next month
2	How old are Jessica and Luke now?	eleven	ten
3	Where is Jessica?	in her room	in Luke's room
4	What is she doing?	She's making a list.	She's writing an e-mail.
5	Where is Jessica and Luke's mum?	in the garden	in the kitchen

2 Before the party

_______ / 6

Draw lines from the sentences to Jessica or Luke.

Jessica

1 ... makes an invitation list.

2 ... makes invitation cards.

3 ... invites the SHoCK Team.

4 ... thinks the SHoCK Team kids are mad.

5 ... writes them an e-mail.

6 ... is hungry.

Luke

3 Food at the party

_______ / 4

What food do Luke and Jessica want at the party? Complete the list.

1 *Luke*   pizza, _____________________, _____________________

2 *Jessica* _____________________, _____________________

LANGUAGE

_______ / 30

1 GRAMMAR The Summers are busy

_______ / 5

Write what they are doing and what they aren't doing.

1 Mum and Dad _________________________________ (work) in the kitchen.

  They _________________________________ (not / work) at the restaurant.

2 Mum _________________________________ (make) a cake.

  But she _________________________________ (not / make) a chocolate cake.

3 Dad _________________________________ (put) chicken legs on the baking tray (= Backblech).

  He _________________________________ (not / put) chips on the baking tray.

4 Jessica and Luke _________________________________ (go) to the shop together.

  They _________________________________ (not / argue).

5 Jessica and Luke _________________________________ (buy) some bottles of orange juice.

  But they _________________________________ (not / buy) any milk.

☞ **Present progressive**
So bildest du das **present progressive**:

| 3. Person Singular | he / she ▶ **is** mak**ing** |
| | he / she ▶ **is**n't putt**ing** |

| 3. Person Plural | they ▶ **are** work**ing** |
| | they ▶ **are**n't argu**ing** |

Darauf musst du achten, wenn du **-ing** an das Verb hängst:
A: Das **-ing** wird einfach angehängt ▶ work**ing**; go**ing**
B: Das stumme **e** fällt weg ▶ mak**ing**; prepar**ing**; argu**ing**
C: Der Konsonant verdoppelt sich nach kurzem Vokal ▶ gett**ing**

2   WORDS Food for the party

_______ / 5

*Fill in **any** or **some**.*

1   *Jessica*   We need ____________ apples and ____________ bananas for a fruit salad.

2   *Luke*   And we haven't got ____________ oranges.

3   *Jessica*   Have we got ____________ biscuits at home?

4   *Luke*   I think we have, but we haven't got ____________ chips.

> **some** oder **any**
>
> **some** ▸ in **bejahten Aussagesätzen**
> **any**   ▸ in **verneinten Aussagesätzen**
> **any**   ▸ in **Fragesätzen**
> **some** ▸ in **Fragesätzen**, in denen du **etwas anbietest** oder um **etwas bittest**

3   GRAMMAR Are they getting ready for the party?

_______ / 5

*Write questions. Use the **present progressive**.*

1   Dan and Jo – read – their – e-mails?

____

2   Jack – phone – his friends?

____

3   Sophie and Ananda – think about – presents?

____

4   Ananda – make – a present?

____

5   Sophie – run – to a shop?

____

> **Present progressive: questions**
> So bildest du Fragen im **present progressive**:
>
> 3. Person Singular   **Is** he / she phon**ing**?
>
> 3. Person Plural   **Are** they read**ing**?
>
> Darauf musst du achten, wenn du **-ing** an das Verb hängst:
> A: Das **-ing** wird einfach angehängt ▸ read**ing**
> B: Das stumme **e** fällt weg ▸ phon**ing**
> C: Der Konsonant verdoppelt sich nach kurzem Vokal ▸ run**ning**

4   GRAMMAR Jack's questions

_______ / 5

Find the right word order for Jack's questions.

1   you – what – doing – are?

____

2   what – you – talking – about?

____

3   Dan – is – doing – what?

____

4   Sophie and Ananda – reading – why – are?

____

5   going – they – where – are – now?

____

> ☞ **Present progressive: questions** with **question word**
>
> So bildest du Fragen mit Fragewort im **present progressive**:
>
> **Fragewort + are / aren't / is + Subjekt + Verb** mit **-ing**
>
> | | |
> |---|---|
> | 2. Person Singular | **What are** you do**ing?** |
> | 3. Person Singular | **Where is** Dan go**ing?** |
> | 3. Person Plural | **Where are** Sophie and Ananda go**ing?** |

5   GRAMMAR A present for Jessica and Luke

_______ / 5

Complete the sentences. Use the object forms of the personal pronouns:

me • you • him (3x) • her (2x) • it • us • them

1 *Sophie*   We need a present for Jessica and Luke. What can we give ___________?

2 *Ananda*   Jessica likes earrings. We can buy ___________ earrings. But what about Luke?

3 *Jack*   We can buy ___________ an earring too. He can wear ___________ in one ear.

4 *Ananda*   Jack is mad. Don't listen to ___________, Sophie.

5 *Jack*   Ananda is boring. Don't listen to ___________, Sophie. Listen to ___________.

My ideas are never boring.

6 *Sophie*   I'm listening to ___________, Jack. But listen to ___________: We think an earring for Luke

isn't a good idea.

7 *Jack*   OK. What can we buy for ___________?

6　WORDS　In the kitchen

_______/5

Look at the picture and find the missing words.

1　You can put milk for the cat in a ______________.

2　Jessica and Luke are buying five ______________ of orange juice.

3　There is a ______________ of water in the fridge.

4　Can I have a ______________ of water? I'm thirsty.

5　We always put fruit in a ______________.

6　There are three ______________ of crisps on the table.

7　Dad is eating a big ______________ of pizza. He is very hungry.

8　The cornflakes are in a ______________.

9　Who is eating cake from my ______________?

10　And where is the cheese? It's still in the shopping ______________.

WRITING

_______/ 20

Hamster Rob is watching the Summer family

Look at the pictures. What can Hamster Rob see? What are the Summers doing?
*What are Hamster Rob's questions? Use the **present progressive**.*

Jessica – not / clean – my cage /
She – tidy – living room

Luke – not / feed – me /
He – lay – table

Mrs Summer – kitchen /
What – she – do? / Make – cake?

Oh! Mr Summer – make –
mess! Now Mr Summer and
Mrs Summer – argue

Look! The guests – come /
They – bring – lots of presents
for Jessica and Luke

Jessica and Luke –
look at the presents /
They – not / look at me

Start like this:　I'm sitting here in my cage. I can see Jessica. Jessica …

Gesamtpunktzahl _______ / 75   Note _______

READING

_______ / 20

Jessica and Luke's birthday party

It's four thirty on Saturday afternoon. Jessica and Luke are in the living room together with their guests.
They are opening their presents. A book for Jessica and a book for Luke from their grandparents.
An MP3 player for Jessica and a model car for Luke from mum and dad. And what have they got from
their friends? A bag of sweets, a CD and funny socks for Luke. Earrings and a CD for Jessica.
5 But what is this? A piece of paper? No, it's a card from the SHoCK Team.

Mrs Summer is passing around plates of cake. The cake is fantastic, but the kids aren't eating.
They are talking about the project. They are listening to Jack now.

Jack   You can all be in this project. I'm the film director[1]. Jo is the cameraman. Brian can be the robber.
       Sophie you're his girlfriend – well, only for the project, of course. The first scene is outside the
10   restaurant. Brian is waiting for you outside the restaurant. He's wearing sunglasses and a black hat.
       Sophie, you're getting off the bus. You're wearing sunglasses too. Jessica and Luke, our two
       detectives, are on the street next to the restaurant. They're watching you. Lisa, Ananda and Jacob,
       you're going into the restaurant. Dan and Eve are coming out of the restaurant ... wait and see.
       Let's eat the cake now.

---

[1] director [dəˈrektə] *Regisseur/in*

1   The birthday party

______/ 3

Fill in the information.

Where?   ___________________________.

Date?   ___________________________.

Time?   ___________________________.

2   What presents have they got?

______/ 4

Luke	
Jessica	

3   The birthday cake

______/ 1

Why aren't the kids eating the birthday cake? Tick the right answer.

		Right	Wrong
1	Because Mrs Summer is passing the plates around.		
2	Because the cake isn't very good.		
3	Because the kids are too busy.		

4   The first scene is …

______/ 2

Two ideas are right. Tick them.

		Right	Wrong
1	… in a restaurant.		
2	… in front of Jessica and Luke's house.		
3	… outside the *Bottle and Bridge*.		
4	… on a Saturday afternoon.		
5	… on a Sunday morning.		

5 The video project ___/10

Lies die Zeilen 8–13 und unterstreiche, welche Rolle die verschiedenen Personen spielen und wo sie sich aufhalten sollen. Verwende für jede Person eine andere Farbe. Schreibe anschließend englische Notizen in die Tabelle (insgesamt 10 Ideen).

Jack	
Jo	
Brian	
Sophie	
Jessica / Luke	
Lisa / Ananada / Jacob	
Dan / Eve	

LANGUAGE ___/35

1 GRAMMAR A great party ___/5

Write what the kids are doing and what they aren't doing.
*Use the **present progressive**.*

1 At four o'clock the guests _________________ (come).

   They _________________ (give) Jessica and Luke their presents.

2 Jessica _________________ (look) at her presents. She _________________ (wear) her new earrings.

3 Luke _________________ (not / wear) new earrings. He _________________ (read) a card.

4 At four thirty Mrs Summer _________________ (pass) around plates of cake, but all the kids

   _________________ (talk) about the video project. They _________________ (not / eat) the cake.

5 At five o'clock they are hungry[1]. They _________________ (eat) the birthday cake now.

---

[1] (to) be hungry ['hʌŋgri] *hungrig sein*

2   GRAMMAR In the kitchen   ____/ 10

Mr Summer is asking lots of questions. Write his questions and Mrs Summer's short answers.

1   kids – eat – cake?

    Mr Summer ____

    Mrs Summer   No, they ___________________.

2   Jessica – wear – earrings?

    Mr Summer ____

    Mrs Summer   Yes, ___________________.

3   Luke – play – model car?

    Mr Summer ____

    Mrs Summer   No, ___________________.

4   The girls – dance?

    Mr Summer ____

    Mrs Summer   Yes, ___________________.

5   You – put – chicken legs – on a plate?

    Mr Summer ____

    Mrs Summer   Yes, ___________________.

> ☞ **Present progressive: questions**
> Wie du Fragen im **present progressive** bildest und was du bei der Schreibung
> beachten musst, kannst du auf der S. 47 nachlesen.

3   GRAMMAR The guests are hungry now   ____/ 5

*Fill in **any** or **some**.*

1   *Jessica*   Would you ___________ fruit salad, Lisa?

2   *Lisa*   Thanks, but I have still got ___________ cake on my plate.

3   *Brian*   But I haven't got ___________ cake on my plate. Can I have ___________ fruit salad, please?

4   *Jacob*   Can I have ___________ fruit salad too, please?

> ☞ **some** oder **any**
>
> **some** ▶ in **bejahten Aussagesätzen**
> **any** ▶ in **verneinten Aussagesätzen**
> **any** ▶ in **Fragesätzen**
> **some** ▶ in **Fragesätzen**, in denen du **etwas anbietest** oder um **etwas bittest**.

4   GRAMMAR Hamster Rob and Hamster Ronnie

Look at Hamster Ronnie's answers. Find the right question word for Hamster Rob's questions. Use:

| What • Where • Why |

1 *Rob*   ___________ are the kids doing?   *Ronnie*   They're dancing the Hokey Cokey.

2 *Rob*   But Luke isn't dancing. ___________ is he doing?   *Ronnie*   He's eating chicken legs.

3 *Rob*   ___________ is Luke eating chicken legs?   *Ronnie*   Because he's hungry.

4 *Rob*   ___________ is Jessica going?   *Ronnie*   She's going outside.

5 *Rob*   ___________ is she going outside?   *Ronnie*   Because somebody is leaving.

5   GRAMMAR The end of the party

_____ / 5

Complete the sentences. Use the object forms of the personal pronouns:

| me • you • him • her • it (2x) • us (2x) • them (2x) |

1 *Dan and Jo*   It's a great party, Luke. Thanks for inviting ___________.

2 *Eve*   There are so many plates and glasses. I can help ___________, Jessica.

3 *Jessica*   Great! You can help ___________ put ___________ in the dishwasher.

4 *Eve*   What about the cake? Where can I put ___________?

5 *Jessica*   Brian loves cake. We can put two pieces in a box for ___________.

6 *Eve*   What about Lisa? Can we give ___________ a piece too?

7 *Jessica*   Yes, of course. You can put ___________ in this small box.

8 *Eve*   Where are all the kids? Let's find ___________ so they can help ___________.

6   WORDS After the party

Find the missing preposition.

| about • for • in (3x) • on • off • at (2x) • with |

Luke is ___________ the kitchen, but he doesn't want to help the others. There are lots of plates

___________ the dishwasher. He is going out and he is ___________ a hurry. He is looking ___________

Jessica and Eve but he isn't helping them. Two minutes later he and Jack are getting ___________ the bus.

The bus stops ___________ Jack's house and they are getting ___________ the bus. Jack and Luke are

having chicken legs ___________ salad ___________ dinner. And what are they talking ___________? –

The second scene of the video project.

GETTING BY IN ENGLISH

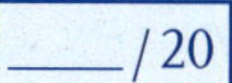

_____ / 20

Ein Anruf von Andrea Kiefer

Während der Geburtstagsparty von Jessica und Luke ruft Andrea aus Deutschland an,
um ihrem Cousin und ihrer Cousine zum Geburtstag zu gratulieren.
Was sagt sie?

Andrea (will alles Gute zum Geburtstag wünschen)

____

Jessica Thank you, Andrea.

Andrea (will wissen, was sie gerade macht)

____

Jessica We're dancing.

Andrea (will wissen, ob Luke auch tanzt)

____

Jessica No, he isn't. He's in the kitchen with Jack. I think they're talking about our project.

Andrea (will wissen, warum sie über ein Projekt sprechen)

____

Jessica We're planning a video project: "The Scary Robbers."
It's a birthday present from the SHoCK Team.

Andrea (sagt, dass das Projekt interessant klingt. Sie will wissen, was Jessica für das Projekt macht.)

____

____

Jessica I'm a detective. Oh, Jack and Luke are coming back to the living room now.

Andrea (will wissen, warum sie ins Wohnzimmer zurückkommen)

____

Jessica I think they want to eat the birthday cake.

Andrea (sagt, dass der Kuchen auch Jessica gehört)

____

Jessica Yes, I know. The boys are eating the cake now. I have to go. I want some cake too!

Unit 5 — Klassenarbeit A

Gesamtpunktzahl _______ / 60   Note _______

LISTENING

_______ / 15

 16 **After the Spring Show**

The Evanses are walking home after the Spring Show. Sam is pushing his sister Sarah in her wheelchair. They are talking about the show with their mum and dad. Listen to Sarah, Sam, Mr Evans and Mrs Evans.

> **New words**
> stage [steidʒ] *Bühne;* prompter ['prɒmptə] *Souffleur, Souffleuse (eine Person, die Schauspielern den Text vorsagt, wenn sie ihn vergessen haben);* (to) prompt [prɒmpt] *soufflieren*

☞ Du kannst diese Aufgabe auch als **Reading**-Aufgabe machen. Den Text findest du auf Seite 37 im **Lösungsheft** abgedruckt.

1 The Spring Show

_______ / 10

Tick the correct box.

		Right	Wrong
1	There was a big box on the ship.	☐	☐
2	Sam was in the box.	☐	☐
3	It was hot inside the box.	☐	☐
4	Sam played the captain.	☐	☐
5	Sam was the prompter.	☐	☐
6	The pirates were big.	☐	☐
7	Sarah wasn't on stage.	☐	☐
8	She was behind the box.	☐	☐
9	She helped the others.	☐	☐
10	It was a beautiful spring evening.	☐	☐

2　Why?

_______/5

Tick the right answer.

	Right	Wrong
1　Why did Mr and Mrs Evans like the show?		
a)　Sarah was a great pirate.	☐	☐
b)　Sam played great music.	☐	☐
c)　The music and the clothes were great.	☐	☐

	Right	Wrong
2　Why did Mr and Mrs Evans laugh?		
a)　The scene was very funny.	☐	☐
b)　Sam was so big and the pirates were so small.	☐	☐
c)　The pirates pulled Sam out of the box.	☐	☐

	Right	Wrong
3　What did Sarah do in the show?		
a)　She was in the choir.	☐	☐
b)　She was a pirate.	☐	☐
c)　She was the prompter.	☐	☐

	Right	Wrong
4　Why was the show scary before the pirates came?		
a)　There were no lights and it was dark.	☐	☐
b)　There was no music.	☐	☐
c)　There were lots of pirates.	☐	☐

	Right	Wrong
5　Why did Mr Evans say goodbye to his family after the show?		
a)　Mr and Mrs Evans have problems.	☐	☐
b)　Mr Evans doesn't like his kids.	☐	☐
c)　Mr Evans went back to London.	☐	☐

LANGUAGE

_______ / 25

1   GRAMMAR   After the Spring Show

_______ / 5

Complete Dan's e-mail to his mum. Use:

> was • were • wasn't • weren't

▶ DanShaw@hotmail.co.uk

Hi Mum,

Our Spring Show _____________ fantastic. We _____________ all very nervous. Jo said he _____________ nervous,

but I know he _____________. And our teacher _____________ nervous too, because there _____________ enough

costumes[1], so two pirates _____________ in jeans. They _____________ happy about that, but it _____________

OK. After the show everybody _____________ happy and tired.

How is everything in New Zealand?

Love, Dan

---

2   GRAMMAR   The Drama Club's report

_______ / 5

Complete Sam's report for the school magazine.
*Use the verbs from the box. Put them in the **simple past**.*

> be (4x) • come • have • look • make • play • say

The Drama Club   *by Sam Evans*

What a great year for the Drama Club! We _____________ lots of rehearsals for the

Spring Show and we _____________ the stage and the pirate ship. Then everything

_____________ ready for the big day. We _____________ very nervous. The band

_____________ and we all _____________ great in our costumes. Lots of our parents

and teachers _____________ to the show. They _____________ that the Spring Show

_____________ fantastic. We _____________ all very happy at the end.

---

[1] costume ['kɔstjuːm] *Kostüm (von Schauspielerinnen und Schauspielern)*

3 GRAMMAR Grandma Scott's questions

_______/5

*Read Luke's answers and write Grandma Scott's questions. Use **was/were**.*

1 (how / show)?

   Grandma ____, Luke?　　*Luke*　It was great.

2 (how many / people / on stage)?

   Grandma ____?　　*Luke*　I think about 40.

3 (you / pirate)?

   Grandma ____?　　*Luke*　Yes, I was.

4 (Jessica / pirate / too)?

   Grandma ____?　　*Luke*　No, she was in the choir.

5 (choir / good)?

   Grandma ____?　　*Luke*　No, it wasn't.

> ☞ Fragen mit **was** oder **were**
>
> 1 Fragen **ohne Fragewort** ▶ **Were** you a pirate?
>   　　　　　　　　　　　　　　 ▶ **Was** she a pirate?
>
> 2 Fragen **mit Fragewort** ▶ **How was** it?

4 GRAMMAR Grandpa Scott's questions

_______/5

*Read Jessica's answers and write Grandpa Scott's questions. Use **did**.*

1 (you / like / your show)?

   Grandpa ____?　*Jessica*　Yes, I did.

2 (you / sing / in the choir)?

   Grandpa ____?　*Jessica*　Yes, I did.

3 (you / sing / alone)?

   Grandpa ____?　*Jessica*　No, I didn't.

4 (you / sing / songs about pirates)?

   Grandpa ____?　*Jessica*　Yes, we did.

5 (somebody / make / a video)?

   Grandpa ____?　*Jessica*　Yes, Dad did.

5 GRAMMAR Pretty Polly has got it all wrong

_______ / 5

Read Polly's sentences. They are all wrong. Write Jack's sentences.

1 **Polly** Your parents didn't watch the show.

   Jack That's wrong, Polly. They _________________________________ the show.

2 **Polly** You didn't play in the band.

   Jack That's wrong, Polly. I _________________________________.

3 **Polly** The pirates didn't get on the ship.

   Jack That's wrong, Polly. The pirates _________________________________.

4 **Polly** But you didn't see the pirates.

   Jack That's wrong, Polly. I _________________________________.

5 **Polly** Your friends didn't like the show.

   Jack That's wrong, Polly. My friends _________________________________.

WRITING

_______ / 20

 ## Sophie's diary

What does Sophie write in her diary about the Spring Show? Look at her ideas and write about the Spring Show.

Sopie's ideas

in the beginning	➜ all the children nervous	suddenly	➜ stage dark
Jack	➜ late	pirates	➜ climb – on ship
two pirates	➜ no costumes (= Kostüme)		➜ I / pirate too ➜ shout
choir	➜ go to wrong part of stage	lights (= Lichter)	➜ go on again
Mr Kingsley	➜ shout	pirates	➜ captain / pull out
	➜ terrible		➜ sing – pirate song
			➜ great
show started	➜ ten minutes late		
stage	➜ fantastic		
first	➜ band – play / choir – sing		
then	➜ Sam / captain / on stage		

Start like this:

Our Spring Show was fantastic, well most of it was fantastic:

Klassenarbeit B

Unit 5

Gesamtpunktzahl _______ / 75   Note ______

READING

____ / 20

International Balloon Festival

Visit the best hot air balloon show in Europe.

Have a weekend of fun in Bristol and watch 150 balloons in all colours and sizes: a big mobile phone or animal balloons.

But balloons aren't the only attraction at the Festival. There are special programmes for kids, go-cart rides[1] and sensational acrobatics.

And there is a spectacular finale on Sunday: 35 balloons light up the night sky to great music and fantastic fireworks. Last year 100,000 people came and watched this show.

For more information about the Festival phone the Festival Information Line on 09068 252 262 (calls @ 60p / min) or check our website www.bristolfiesta.co.uk

Parking: Clifton Lodge Parking or Kennel Lodge Parking at £5 per car.
Train station: Bristol Temple Meads

1 Find the German meaning

____ / 8

Kreuze an, wie du diese Wörter erschließen kannst. Manchmal treffen auch zwei Kästchen zu.
Schreibe dann das deutsche Wort in die rechte Spalte.

englisches Wort	Hinweis aus dem Bild	deutschem Wort ähnlich	bekanntes Wort enthalten	aus dem Zusammenhang	deutsche Bedeutung
international	☐	☐	☐	☐	
hot air balloon	☐	☐	☐	☐	
attraction	☐	☐	☐	☐	
sensational acrobatics	☐	☐	☐	☐	
spectacular finale	☐	☐	☐	☐	
(to) light up	☐	☐	☐	☐	

[1] go-cart ride [raid] *Go-Kart Fahrt*

2   Facts about the Bristol International Balloon Festival ______ / 5

Tick the correct answer(s).

1	When is the Balloon Festival?	in spring		in the evening		at a weekend	
2	How can you get there?	by car		by train		by balloon	
3	How can you get more information?	on the radio		on the internet		by phone	

3   Right – Wrong – Not in the text ______ / 7

Tick the correct box.

		Right	Wrong	Not in the text
1	All balloons are round.			
2	Balloons are in the air at daytime only.			
3	Tickets are expensive.			
4	Parking is free[1].			
5	A phone call is £ 5.			
6	Go-cart rides are free for kids.			
7	Lots of people come and watch.			

LANGUAGE ______ / 35

1   GRAMMAR Where were they? ______ / 10

*Ask questions with **was** or **were** and write the short answers.*

> Jo and Dan / International Balloon Festival?   – Yes
>
> *Were Dan and Jo at the International Balloon Festival?   – Yes, they were.*

1   The Hansons / swimming-pool?   – No

____

2   Jack / rehearsal?   – Yes

____

3   Jack's mother / Mr Green's room?   – Yes

____

____

4   Mr Hanson / garden?   – No

____

5   You / Spring Show?   – No

____

[1] free *kostenlos*

2   GRAMMAR What did they do?

_____/ 10

*Ask questions with **did** and write short answers.*

> Mr Hanson / go / International Balloon Festival?   – No
>
> *Did Mr Hanson go to the International Balloon Festival?   – No, he didn't.*

1   Dan and Jo / go in a balloon?   – No

____

2   Dan and Jo / see / Ananda?   – Yes

____

3   Ananda / have / picnic / with parents?   – No

____

____

4   Ananda's parents / like / the balloons?   – Yes

____

5   You / go / International Balloon Festival?   – No

____

____

3   GRAMMAR Dan's e-mail to Jack

_____/ 5

Complete Dan's e-mail.
*Use the verbs from the box. Put them in the **simple past**.*

> be (3x) • get • go (2x) • have • talk • tell • watch

> ► DanShaw@hotmail.co.uk
>
> Hi Jack,
>
> We ____________ a great time at the International Balloon Festival. We ____________ there by bike.
>
> There ____________ lots of balloons in all colours. We ____________ to the owner[1] of one of the balloons.
>
> He ____________ us a lot of interesting things about balloons. We ____________ how he ____________
>
> his balloon ready. Then there ____________ a big flame[2] and it ____________ up into the sky.
>
> It ____________ fantastic!
>
> Dan

[1] owner ['əʊnə] *Besitzer/in*   [2] flame [fleɪm] *Flamme*

4   GRAMMAR After the International Balloon Festival

_______/5

Complete Dan's sentences. Use the **simple past**.

1 *Ananda*   Did you go to the International Balloon Festival?

   Dan   Yes, I did. I ___________________ (go) there with Jo on Saturday.

2 *Ananda*   I didn't see you there.

   Dan   But we ___________________ (see) you and your parents.

3 *Ananda*   Did you sit on the hill (= Hügel)?

   Dan   No, we didn't. We ___________________ (sit) on a wall (= Mauer) near the balloons.

4 *Ananda*   Did you get information about the balloons?

   Dan   Yes, we did. We ___________________ (get) lots of information from the
owner (= Besitzer/in) of one of the balloons.

5 *Ananda*   What did you do after the Balloon Festival?

   Dan   We phoned Jack and we ___________________ (have) a picnic together.

5   PRONUNCIATION Verbs in the simple past

_______/5

Put the verbs in the simple past and write them in the correct list.

add • answer • climb • hate • hope • play • report • show • start • watch

called [kɔːld]	
painted ['peɪntɪd]	

GETTING BY IN ENGLISH

_____ / 20

After the International Balloon Festival

You and your family are staying in a hotel in Bristol. One evening you go the Balloon Festival.
Later you meet a boy in your hotel. His name is David, he's from London and he only speaks English.
Your brother Leon doesn't speak English. Help him and David.

Leon   Frag ihn, ob er auch beim Balloon Festival war.

You   ____

David   Yes, my parents and I went there yesterday.

You   Ja, er sagt, dass ____

Leon   Frag ihn, ob es ihm gefallen hat.

You   ____

David   It was great! Did you see the acrobatics?

You   Er fand es toll. Er fragt, ob ____

Leon   Sag ihm, dass ich die toll fand.

You   My brother says ____

David   Did you go on the go-karts?

Leon   Was fragt er?

You   Er will wissen, ob ____

We wanted to, but it was too expensive.

Leon   Was erzählst du ihm?

You   Ich habe gesagt, dass ____

David   I think the bands were good. Did you like them?

You   Er sagt, ____

und fragt, ____

Leon   Sag ihm, dass die erste schrecklich war, aber die zweite gut war.

You   ____

Unit 6 Klassenarbeit A

Gesamtpunktzahl _______ / 60   Note _______

LISTENING

_____ / 20

🎧 19 **Bristol – five attractions**

a presentation by Luke Summer

Listen to Luke's presentation.

> **New words**
> attraction [əˈtrækʃn] *Sehenswürdigkeit, Attraktion;* helium gas balloon [ˈhiːliəm gæs bəˈluːn] *Helium-Ballon;* luxury liner [ˈlʌkʃəriˈlaɪnə] *Luxus-Schiff;* (to) design [dɪˈzaɪn] *entwerfen, planen;* a little *ein bisschen*

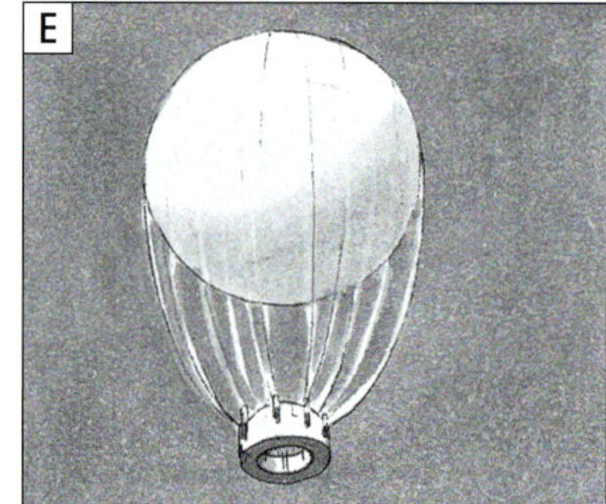

> ☞ Du kannst diese Aufgabe auch als **Reading**-Aufgabe machen. Den Text findest du auf Seite 43 im **Lösungsheft** abgedruckt.

1 What do the pictures show?

_____ / 5

Find the right letter.

1 Bristol Downs	
2 Clifton Suspension Bridge	
3 Galleries Shopping Centre	
4 High Point	
5 *SS Great Britain*	

2 Luke's pictures

_____ / 5

Put the pictures in the right order. Find the right letter.

First picture	Second picture	Third picture	Fourth picture	Last picture

3 Five different places   ____ / 10

Match the letters and the numbers. Be careful. Two letters don't match.

Bristol Downs	1
Clifton Suspension Bridge	2
Galleries Shopping Centre	3
High Point	4
SS Great Britain	5

A   Isambard Kingdom Brunel designed it

B   there is Food Street

C   takes 30 people up 150 metres

D   makes you look down 70 metres

E   is a museum

F   you can play football

G   is in Castle Park

H   is the big bridge in Bristol

I   is a country park

J   is 150 years old

K   you can play there with kites

L   is a helium gas balloon

LANGUAGE   ____ / 20

1 GRAMMAR Shopping   ____ / 5

Simple present or present progressive? Underline the correct verb form.

1   Sophie usually **goes / is going** shopping with her mum, but today she **goes / is going** shopping with Ananda.

2   Ananda and Sophie are at the Galleries Shopping Centre. They **look / are looking** at clothes. Sophie often **buys / is buying** her clothes at the Galleries, but Ananda **doesn't go / isn't going** there very often.

3   Ananda's mother sometimes **makes / is making** dresses for Ananda, but she **doesn't make / isn't making** jeans or T-shirts for her.

4   Ananda **doesn't wear / isn't wearing** a dress today. She is wearing jeans and she **looks for / is looking for** a nice T-shirt or a sweatshirt.

5   So the two girls **look at / are looking at** T-shirts and sweatshirts now.

2   WORDS At the Galleries Shopping Centre   ____/10

a)   *Use **this** or **these** and the correct pronouns.*

Example: *I like this top here. Can I buy it?*

1   What about ___________ sweatshirt? ___________'s nice too.

2   ___________ shoes are great. How much are ___________?

3   I like the colour of ___________ shirt. ___________'s my favourite colour.

4   I like ___________ shoes. Are ___________ expensive?

5   ___________ dress is really pretty. How much is ___________?

b)   *Use **that** or **those** and the correct pronouns.*

Example: *That T-shirt there is cool. I'd like to buy it!*

1   ___________ top in the magazine is really pretty. Is ___________ expensive?

2   ___________ socks are funny. I'd like to buy ___________ for Luke.

3   I don't like ___________ shirt – ___________'s too big.

4   Look at ___________ boots. ___________'re really great.

5   I don't like ___________ dress because ___________'s purple.

3   GRAMMAR The International Balloon Festival in Bristol   ____/5

*Use the **simple past**.*

1   Last week there ___________ (be) the International Balloon Festival at Ashton Court Bristol.

2   Lots of people ___________ (be) there and the Summer family ___________ (go) there too.

3   Luke and Jessica ___________ (see) lots and lots of balloons.

4   Mr Summer ___________ (take) photos and the kids ___________ (have) ice cream.

5   Mrs Summer ___________ (not / have) ice cream.

6   She ___________ (go) to a nice place under a tree.

7   She ___________ (sit) down and ___________ (make) some sandwiches.

GETTING BY IN ENGLISH

_____ / 20

At the Galleries Shopping Centre

You are at the Galleries Shopping Centre. You meet Sophie and Ananda.

Du willst wissen,

... wie oft sie hier einkaufen gehen?

____

... was sie hier normalerweise kaufen?

____

... ob Kleidung hier sehr teuer ist?

____

... ob sie dir ein Geschäft zeigen können, wo man Souvenirs (= souvenirs) kaufen kann?

____

... wann ihre Sommerferien anfangen?

____

... ob sie an der Schule Deutsch lernen?

____

... ob du ein Foto von ihnen machen darfst?

____

Du willst sagen, dass

... du ihnen die Fotos schicken kannst.

____

.... du Bristol aus vielen Gründen magst.

____

... du in einem kleinen Dorf in Deutschland wohnst.

____

Unit 6   Klassenarbeit B

Gesamtpunktzahl ______ / 60   Note ______

READING

____ / 15

An e-mail from Germany

▸ JessicaSummer@hotmail.co.uk

Hi Mum, hi Dad,

Yesterday we went to a small village near Neuss. Andrea's friend Susanne lives there on a farm with her parents. We went there by bus and we walked from the bus station to the farm. It's a beautiful farm. There is a river[1], a small bridge and an old tower. Susanne showed us the tower and we explored the place. Andrea found a big box.

5   Susanne and I opened the box. In the box there were lots of old toys. Susanne took four little boats from the box. We took them to the river and played with them there under the bridge. Luke hurt his leg when he climbed on the bridge. Then we went back to the farm house. Luke smiled again when he saw the big chocolate cake on the table. We all had a piece of it – it was great. It's six o'clock now and Aunt Jane is making dinner. I'm looking forward[2] to it because Aunt Jane always makes really good food.

10   I hope everything is OK with you.

Love, Jessica

1   The farm

____ / 5

Tick the correct box.

		Right	Wrong	Not in the text
1	The farm is in Neuss.			
2	Three people live on the farm.			
3	There is an old tower on the farm.			
4	The farm is old.			
5	You can't walk to the farm from the bus station.			

2   The children

____ / 7

Who did what? Tick the right name.

		Andrea	Jessica	Luke	Susanne
1	... showed the kids the tower				
2	... found a box				
3	... opened the box				
4	... took boats from the box				
5	... hurt his leg				
6	... looks forward to dinner				

[1] river ['rɪvə] *Fluss*   [2] (to) look forward to sth. ['fɔːwəd] *sich auf etwas freuen*

3 What did the children do together ...?

_____/ 3

Complete the sentences. Use the verbs in the **simple past**.

1 ... in the tower?   They ____.

2 ... at the river?   They ____.

3 ... in the farm house?   They ____.

LANGUAGE

_____/ 25

1 WORDS Old toys

_____/ 10

Use:

> this • that • these • those

1 _Andrea_   Look at ___________ little teddy bears. Aren't they nice?

2 _Jesssica_   I like ___________ bear, but I don't like ___________ bear. It hasn't got any legs.

3 _Luke_   I like ___________ boats. ___________ old bears are for girls.

4 _Susanne_   All ___________ toys must be very old.

       We can take ___________ bear and ___________ little boat.

5 _Luke_   Why don't we take ___________ four boats and put ___________ bears back in the box?

2 GRAMMAR Under the bridge

_____/ 10

Complete the sentences with the ideas from the box. Be careful about the word order.

> 1 kids / took / boats / river
> 2 each boat / in the wind / sailed[1]
> 3 she saw / that / there / a hole[2] / her boat / was
> 4 it / had / big sail[3]
> 5 they / hungry / were

1 It was windy when ____

2 But the kids enjoyed it because ____________________________________

3 Only Andrea was sad when ____

____

4 Luke's boat was very good because __________________________________

5 They went back to the farm house because ____________________________

[1] sailed [seild] _segelte_   [2] hole [həʊl] _Loch_   [3] a sail [seil] _ein Segel_

3   GRAMMAR The Kiefer family

_____/ 5

a)   *Use the **present progressive** and complete the sentences.*

1   It's 7.30 pm. Mr Kiefer ___________________________ (sit) in front of the TV.

2   Tonight he ___________________________ (watch) a football match. Eintracht Frankfurt

___________________________ (play) Dynamo Dresden.

3   Mrs Kiefer and Andrea ___________________________ (not / watch) TV. They

___________________________ (make) a chocolate cake.

b)   *Use the **simple present** and complete the sentences.*

1   Mrs Kiefer ___________________________ (not / like) football. In the evenings she often

___________________________ (go) jogging with a friend.

2   Andrea and Mr Kiefer sometimes ___________________________ (watch) a football match together.

3   Mr Kiefer ___________________________ (watch) lots of football matches and he

___________________________ (play) football in a club.

WRITING

_____/ 20

Mrs Summer's e-mail

Read Jessica's e-mail again (p. 70). Now write Mrs Summer's e-mail. She is worried. She asks about Luke's leg.
She wants to know more about Andrea's friend Susanne, about the farm, about the river, the bridge,
the tower and the old box.

Here are some ideas:

Luke
How is …?
What …?
Why did you …?

Susanne
How old …?
Animals on farm?
How big / bridge?
Why / play / there?
Why tower on farm?
How old tower?

Start like this:

Hi Jessica, hi Luke,

…

Speaking

SPEAKING

_____ / 20

WELCOME

02 Jessica and Moritz

Höre dir die Unterhaltung zwischen Jessica Summer und Moritz Müller zweimal an.

03 Jessica and you

Jessica möchte sich mit dir unterhalten. Drücke die Pausentaste nach jeder Frage und antworte auf ihre Frage. Dies ist eine Sprechübung. Du musst also nichts aufschreiben.

Jessica	Hi, my name is Jessica. What's your name?
You	…
Jessica	Oh, that's a nice name. Can you spell it for me?
You	…
Jessica	I'm from England. Where are you from?
You	…
Jessica	I'm eleven. How old are you?
You	…
Jessica	My favourite colour is black. What's your favourite colour?
You	…
Jessica	My favourite day is Friday. What's your favourite day?
You	…
Jessica	I'm at Cotham School. It's a nice school and it's a big school. What about your school?
You	…
Jessica	My telephone number is 52447806. What's your telephone number?
You	…
Jessica	Goodbye and good luck with your new school.
You	…

Lerntipp   So kannst du **Speaking Skills** üben:

- Lerne den Dialog zwischen Jessica und Moritz auswendig.
- Mache deinen Dialog mit Jessica noch einmal.
- Nimm deinen Dialog auf (Handy / Computer …).
- Übe den Dialog mit deinen Eltern, einer Freundin oder einem Freund.
- Lies einen Dialog im Englischbuch, bis du ihn flüssig sprechen kannst.

SPEAKING

_____ / 20

UNIT 1

🎧 05 Luke

Luke spricht über seine neue Klasse, seine Lehrer und seine Fächer. Höre Luke zu.
Luke is talking about his new class, his teachers and his subjects. Listen to Luke.

I'm in Form 7JM. There are fifteen boys and seventeen girls. I've got two new friends – Brian and Dan.
Brian is eleven and Dan is twelve. They're from Bristol and they're nice. Our teachers are nice too.
Mr Morton is our English teacher and Mr Clark is our PE teacher. English and PE are my favourite
subjects. Mr Morton is our form teacher too. Our timetable is OK. School starts at 8.45 and my first lesson
on Monday is Science. There is a morning break at 10.45 and a lunch break at 12.40. On Mondays the two
lessons after lunch are Geography and Music. The end of school is at 3.30.

🎧 06 Your new form

Jetzt sprichst du über deine Klasse, deine Freunde und Freundinnen, deine Lehrer und Lehrerinnen
und deine Fächer. Du kannst dir zuerst Stichpunkte notieren. Die Tabelle hilft dir.

my form	
boys / girls	
new friends	
teachers / form teachers	
favourite subjects	
timetable	

Lerntipp	So kannst du **Speaking Skills** üben:

- ☐ Höre dir Lukes Ausführungen noch einmal an.
- ☐ Lerne Lukes Ausführungen auswendig.
- ☐ Sprich über deine Klasse, deine Freunde, Lehrer und Fächer, bis du so flüssig sprechen kannst wie Luke.

SPEAKING

UNIT 2

🎧 08 Family, pets and weekends

Listen to Sam Evans. He talks about his family, pets and weekends.

Hi,

I'm Sam Evans. I'm 15. I've got a sister, but I haven't got a brother. My sister's name is Sarah. She's 11. We're from Bristol. We live in a flat with our mum. Mum and Dad aren't together. They're divorced.

We haven't got pets, but Dad has got a dog. I love dogs, but our flat is too small for dogs.

Weekends are nice for Sarah and me. I get up late, phone friends, watch TV or play computer games. Sarah gets up late too. Every Saturday she goes to her friends or her friends come to our house. They sit and talk and sometimes they watch a film. Mum sometimes works at the weekend. She works in a shop and lots of shops open on Saturdays and Sundays. When she doesn't work we sometimes go to the park together.

🎧 09 My family

Now it's your turn. Complete the mind map and talk about your family, pets and weekends.
Nun bist du dran. Vervollständige die Mindmap und sprich über deine Familie, Haustiere und Wochenenden.

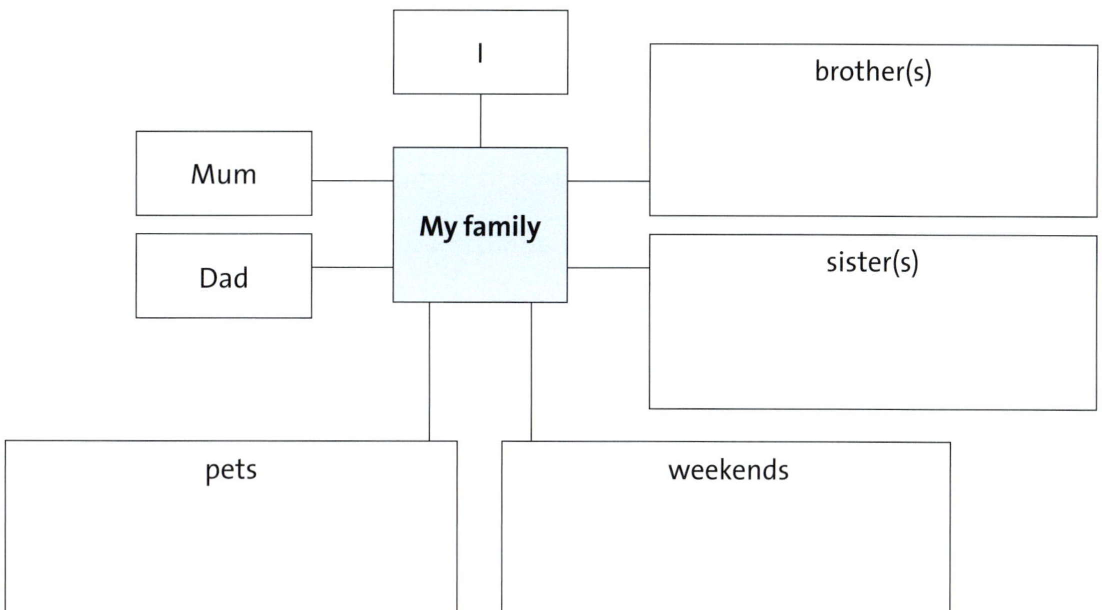

Lerntipp	So kannst du **Speaking Skills** üben:

- Höre dir Sams Ausführungen an und lies dabei leise mit.
- Zeichne in den Text ein, wo Sam Betonungen setzt (') und wo er einzelne Wörter verbindet (⌢).
- Lies den Text zusammenhängend und mit Betonungen.
- Sprich über deine Familie und achte dabei auf Betonung und flüssigen Vortrag.

SPEAKING

______ / 20

UNIT 3

🎧 11 **Jessica: The 9 to 13 Club – A new sports club for kids**

Listen to Jessica.

🎧 12 **You: The 9 to 13 Club – A new sports club for kids**

Talk about the 9 to 13 Club.
Jetzt erzähle du, was du aus der Broschüre an Information über den 9 to 13 Club weitergeben kannst.

The 9 to 13 Club

The Sports Club for kids
15 Spring Street

Office opening hours   **Mon / Wed / Fri 2.00 – 5.00 pm**

Phone 702314

Kids 9 – 13

Football training (boys)	Mon / Thu 4.00 – 5.00 pm
Hockey (girls)	Fri 5.00 – 6.00 pm
Hockey (boys)	Fri 6.00 – 7.00 pm
Aerobics (girls)	Tue / Wed 4.00 – 5.00 pm
Break dancing (boys)	Tue / Wed 6.00 – 7.00 pm

Special Holiday Offers   for more information phone our office

3-day horse riding course
Weekend family hike

Here is some help:

There is …
Office opening hours are …
Football / hockey / … training is on …
On … girls can …
On … boys can …
There are two special holiday offers: …

Lerntipp	So kannst du **Speaking Skills** üben:

☐ Höre dir Jessicas Ausführungen noch einmal an und sprich leise mit.
☐ Achte dabei besonders auf Jessicas Aussprache.
☐ Achte beim Sprechen besonders auf die Aussprache einzelner Wörter.

SPEAKING

_______ / 20

UNIT 4

🎧 14 What are they doing?

Look at the picture and listen to Jessica and Luke.

🎧 15 Now you

Answer Jessica's questions.
Drücke die Pausentaste, damit du Zeit für deine Antwort hast.

Jessica	Is Brian in the restaurant?	_You_	…
Jessica	Is he wearing sunglasses?	_You_	…
Jessica	What is Sophie doing? Is she going into the restaurant?	_You_	…
Jessica	Is she wearing sunglasses?	_You_	…
Jessica	Is somebody coming out of the restaurant?	_You_	…
Jessica	What about Eve? Has she got a bag?	_You_	…
Jessica	Where are Jack and Jo?	_You_	…
Jessica	Have they got the video camera?	_You_	…
Jessica	Are they doing the first scene?	_You_	…

Lerntipp So kannst du **Speaking Skills** üben:

- Höre dir den Dialog zwischen Jessica und Luke noch einmal an. (Track 14)
- Sprich Jessicas Fragen nach. Achte dabei auf ihre Satzmelodie (= Intonation).
  - ➜ Drücke die Pausentaste nach jeder Frage (Track 14).
- Sprich Lukes Antworten nach. Achte dabei auf seine Satzmelodie (= Intonation).
  - ➜ Drücke die Pausentaste nach jeder Antwort (Track 14).
- Höre dir Track 15 noch einmal an und drücke die Pausentaste nach Jessicas Fragen.
- Sprich deine Antworten. Achte dabei auf deine Satzmelodie (= Intonation).

SPEAKING

_____ / 20

UNIT 5

🎧 17 **What did you do last weekend?**

Grandma Scott asks Luke what he did last weekend. Listen to Grandma Scott and Luke.

🎧 18 **Now you**

Make notes of what you did last weekend. Then answer Grandma Scott's questions.
Tell her what you did last weekend.
Drücke die Pausentaste nach jeder Frage, damit du Zeit für deine Antwort hast.

Grandma	Last Saturday I got up at seven o'clock and went for a walk in the park. There weren't many people because it was so early. Then I had breakfast with Grandpa. When did you get up? Did you get up early too?
You	...
Grandma	What did you do in the morning?
You	...
Grandma	Did you have lunch at home?
You	...
Grandma	What did you do after lunch?
You	...
Grandma	And in the evening? What did you do in the evening? Did you watch TV?
You	...
Grandma	Did you go to bed late?
You	...

Lerntipp   So kannst du **Speaking Skills** üben:

- Höre dir den Dialog zwischen Großmutter und Luke noch einmal an. (Track 17)
- Sprich Großmutters Aussagen und Fragen nach.
  ➜ Drücke jedesmal die Pausentaste, wenn Großmutter gesprochen hat. (Track 17)
- Sprich Lukes Antworten nach.
  ➜ Drücke die Pausentaste nach jeder Antwort. (Track 17)
- Höre dir Track 18 noch einmal an und drücke die Pausentaste nach Großmutters Fragen.
- Sprich deine Antworten, bis du sie so flüssig kannst wie Luke.

SPEAKING

_____ / 20

UNIT 6

🔊 20 Neuss – a German town

Andrea Kiefer lives in Neuss. She talks about Neuss and asks you about your town.
Listen to her and answer her questions.

> 👉 Höre dir Andreas Ausführungen zuerst einmal an. Sammle dann Ideen, wie du Andreas
> Fragen beantworten kannst. Höre dir Andreas Ausführungen ein zweites Mal an.
> Drücke dabei die Pausentaste nach jeder Frage, damit du Zeit für deine Antwort hast.

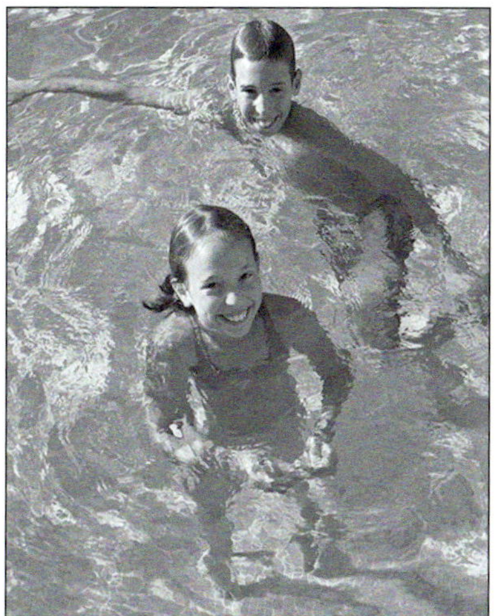

outdoor[1] and indoor[2]
swimming pool

ride bike
play football

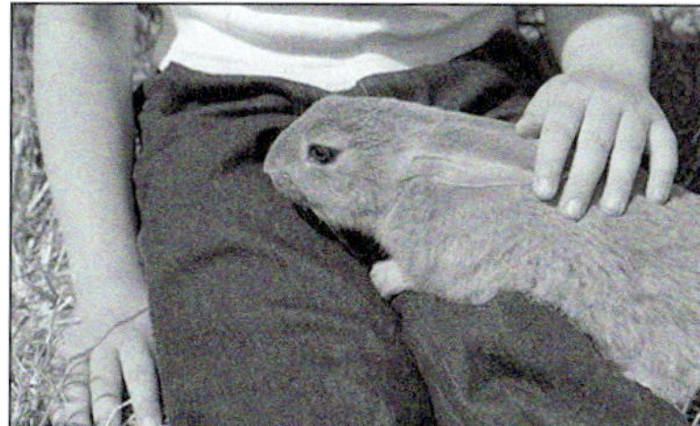

Children's Farm
Chocolate Museum Cologne[3]

Andrea's questions	Your ideas
What about you? Where do you live?	
What are the things you can do in your town?	
What about your town? What makes your town special?	
Which interesting places are near your town?	

[1] outdoor ['autdɔː] *außen*   [2] indoor ['ɪndɔː] *innen*   [3] Cologne [kə'loʊn] *Köln*

Neuss – a German town

Andrea	Hi! I'm Andrea and I live in Neuss. Neuss is a town in Germany near Düsseldorf. What about you? Where do you live?
You	…
Andrea	I like Neuss because there are lots of things you can do there. Our South Park swimming pool is great. There is a swimming pool inside and outside. It's open in the summer and winter. I like swimming so I often go there with my friends. What things can you do in your town?
You	…
Andrea	Cool! And another great thing about Neuss: It has got a really big park. You can do lots of things there. You can ride your bike, you can play football and other games and you can climb the big trees. And in summer there are shows for kids! It's really great. What about your town? Why do you like it?
You	…
Andrea	There are lots of interesting things near Neuss. You can go to the Children's Farm. At the Children's Farm kids can learn about farm life and there is the Chocolate Museum in Cologne where you can learn about chocolate and eat lots of chocolate too. That's a lot of fun. Which interesting places are near your town?
You	…

Lerntipp   So kannst du **Speaking Skills** üben:

- Höre dir Andreas Ausführungen noch einmal an. Achte dabei auf ihre Aussprache.
- Sprich Andreas Ausführungen und Fragen nach. Versuche dabei, Andreas Aussprache nachzuahmen.
  → Drücke jedesmal die Pausentaste, wenn Andrea gesprochen hat.
- Unterstreiche im Text Ausdrücke, die dir bei Andreas Ausführungen gefallen haben.
- Sammle Ideen über deine Stadt und sprich dann darüber. Versuche dabei, flüssig und zusammenhängend zu sprechen.
  → Drücke jedesmal die Pausentaste, wenn Andrea gesprochen hat.